Michèle Ray

THE TWO SHORES
OF HELL

JOHN MURRAY

Translated by
Elizabeth Abbott and Shirley Deane

First published in Great Britain 1968
by John Murray, Albemarle Street, London
and printed by The Camelot Press Ltd.,
London and Southampton
7195 1826 1

To the G.I.s and the Vietcong,
my friends

Acknowledgments

I wish to thank M. Figuier of the Etablissements A.L.G.A. By lending me a 16 mm Beaulieu electric camera, he made it possible for me to make my film. And, of course, my thanks to the Renault Company.

M. R.

Contents

Illustrations

PART I

With the Americans

I

Saigon

The Boeing has just taken off from Hong Kong. The most beautiful bay in the world leaves the passengers indifferent, blasé. I am the only one trying not to miss anything of the superb view vanishing into the mist. I'm apparently calm, but my stomach is beginning to tighten. Three short hours—then Saigon, Vietnam and war, the Vietcong, and atrocities, bombs. . . .

My imagination races and the ball of fear in my stomach is swelling. For six months I've been preparing for, thinking about, this story.

Now the end's in sight and suddenly I have stage-fright.

'Fasten your seat belts—we're coming down at Saigon.'

If Hong Kong left the passengers cold, Vietnam wakes them up and stirs their curiosity: we are flying over the heart of the world's news. Everyone cranes forward. All eyes are riveted on the windows and the little tip of Indo-China that can be seen—though barely—through the clouds.

I imagine their thoughts:

The G.I. returning from leave: 'Still six more months to fight!'

The business man: 'If only it lasts!'

The Vietnamese: 'Our unhappy country, at war for so long!'

As for the others, the tourists, they will be able to say: 'I flew over Vietnam. I stayed an hour in transit at Tan Son Nhut.'

Perhaps at that point they'll manage to interest their audience, who have dozed through the account of their visit to Angkor or the hanging gardens of Japan.

The rice fields come nearer, the houses take shape, the chatter grows louder . . . and at last, the runway.

A part of the gigantic American war machine unrolls beneath us at 200 miles an hour. Bombers, jet and prop fighters, fat-bellied freighters, small planes, huge planes, middle-sized planes.

We roll slowly towards the *parking*. Everywhere, on planes, huts,

crates—stencilled in great, black letters: U.S. Army. It is the trademark of Vietnam today. The airfield is a permanent exhibition of
every type of equipment made by American industry.

The Constellations with an enormous disc on top—radar—amaze
me. . . . The trolleys being pushed along—with bombs and rockets
instead of harmless suitcases—fascinate me. I don't want to miss
any of it, I want my mind to register everything. I am avid. I want
to know.

The cabin door opens, the steps come forward: the heat and humi-
dity beat down on us. The field is flooded: it is the rainy season.

Hostesses in Vietnamese tunics of turquoise-blue, white trousers,
beautiful and slender as reeds, welcomed us, smiling. They spoke
softly, with charm, and tranquillity. Two fighters taking off with a
great roar made me jump, but left the M.P.s on duty unmoved.
Slouched on one hip, hands resting on revolver butts, munching the
eternal chewing-gum, they preferred to eye the passengers. Perhaps
trying to spot a female figure which would remind them of their
girl-friend back home.

'Michèle Ray? I'm Gerard Py.'

Lartéguy had warned me: 'Gerard is a veteran. A cameraman
for C.B.S., it's his second war in Vietnam. He'll be able to help you.
But take a tip: never refuse to have dinner with him. He's a fabulous
cook, and he loves to treat his friends.'

'I haven't got a visa. Too long and difficult to get one in Paris.
How much should I declare? And my gear? And the hotel? And
what if I'm sent back?'

I spoke too fast. I swamped him with questions.

'That's no problem. Nearly all of us arrive without visas. Get a
seventy-two hour transit. We'll arrange to extend it afterwards.'

The queue, forms to fill in, and still more forms, the raised eye-
brow of the immigration officer:

'Seventy-two hour visa granted.'

To the customs men:

'No, no—I'm not armed!'

Suitcases loaded on a taxi, and my first brush with Saigon traffic.

Jammed for an hour between an enormous truck and a jeep, I
heard about my first Top Priority problem in the middle of a concert
of warning honks and backfiring engines.

A symphony of colours with the green of military vehicles pre-
dominating; and red—the Hondas of the long-haired Vietnamese;
and blue—old 4-horse-power taxis which went heaven knows how,
with doors and boot tied on by wire. The latest American models
with glittering paintwork, a swarm of bikes with Vietnamese ladies
in long, flowing robes pedalling gracefully, if precariously. The
traditional two-wheeled pedicabs too, of course: with pedals or
with motor, darting everywhere. Giving way to traffic on the right
no longer exists. Since the fall of Diem, the municipal police have
lost their authority: no one takes any notice of their white helmets,
the mechanical gestures which are useless, controlling nothing.

The noise, the colours, the heat, red lights that everyone ignores.
Driving in Saigon is an adventure already.

'You could come to my place, or to one of the French Press boys.
But it complicates things: you being a respectable girl!'

'I'm shattered!'

'Don't mention it! We'll try to ferret out a hotel for you!'

Rue Tu Do, once rue Catinat, where—it seems—it's all happening—the Continental, the Majestic, the Caravelle . . . booked out.

After several refusals in hotels reserved for Americans—you know
them by their anti-grenade gratings and M.P.s on guard—I finally
found a room . . . with five beds!

Towards midnight when the G.I.s came back—commotion,
banging at the door! Panicking, I suddenly asked myself if I'd
really booked all five beds!

Impossible to sleep: for the first time I heard cannon fue. It
thunders every night. Subconsciously perhaps, I was waiting for a
grenade to explode, some outrage near at hand. I still had the
mentality of a 'new chum'. Though I didn't see a Vietcong behind
each tree, danger's always with you in Saigon, a permanent sense of
insecurity.

But you get used to it. Looking back, I can hardly believe that I
actually said: 'Heaven knows what might happen: give me your
telephone number!'

Three thousand piastres for the room! A night's shelter at Ritz
prices!

My first visit to the Agence France-Presse (A.F.P.): five Frenchmen. I had a great welcome, but they still weren't sure whether they
ought to be pleased by my coming, or scornful:

'What's a nice girl like you doing here?'

For the mail of journalists in transit, a folder labelled: 'Blood-sucking correspondents of the A.F.P.'

What they didn't know was that I had a little dossier on each one of them: four or five very funny lines!

With Gerard—also called Fatty—always behind or in front, I set about getting myself accredited.

At the Vietnamese Press Office, I had to fill in umpteen forms after presenting my letter of introduction from the *Nouvel Observateur*. As for my demand for an extended visa, I received three days later a letter certifying that my demand had been noted.

This bit of paper would do until I got the final visa—usually, it seems, on the day the visa expires. The provisional visa obviously makes it easier to kick people out of the country. Now that I held two Vietnamese press cards, one civil, the other military, a letter— that I never used—to penetrate as far as Tan Son Nhut, and a police pass for the curfew, I could go and see the Americans.

At the Special Projects Office of the M.A.C.V. (Military Assistant Command in Vietnam) Colonel Hunt, the press attaché, welcomed me.

In six months, the Special Projects Office has accredited 1,100 journalists. The permanent corps of the foreign press in Vietnam, including television technicians, has about 400 members. Their tour of duty is generally one year. The others are classed as 'tourists': tourists who even come at times in organized groups with guides and interpreters. After staying for various lengths of time, often less than a week, they go back to their own countries as 'specialists on Vietnam'.

More forms, of course, more photographs as well, and a cable to my paper asking them to confirm my assignment. Three days after my arrival, I had the open sesame: the M.A.C.V. press card.

The bearer of this card should be accorded full co-operation and assistance, within the bounds of operational requirements and military security, to assure successful completion of his mission. The bearer is authorized to receive rations and quarters on a re-imbursable basis. Upon presentation of this card, the bearer is entitled to receive air, water and ground transport under a No. 3 priority, but only within the Republic of Vietnam. A signed flight release is on file in the M.A.C.V. Office of Information.

With all my papers in order, I was therefore allowed to attend my first briefing at what the reporters call the 'five o'clock follies'!

Every afternoon, at 1700 hours, the journalists are given a résumé and a report. The operations of the past twenty-four hours are announced, commented on, and analysed by sheet codes, figures, initials, all of them incomprehensible to the uninitiated. It is a language of its own, with words that exist only in Vietnam, like *klik* for kilometre.

The press conference is held in the building of the J.U.S.P.A.O., another barbarous term meaning Joint United States Public Affairs Office. It is at the same time a unified press service for the three forces—four counting the Marines—and for the civil administration, plus a propaganda centre and the bureau of psychological warfare. It's almost like a ministry, protected as it is by barricades of sand-bags, guarded by soldiers, sub-machine-guns at the ready, in the very heart of the city, at the corner of Boulevards Nguyen Hue and Le Loi, the old Boulevard Charner. To get in, you have to show the M.P.s your credentials. In the conference room, obviously too small, firstcomers take the armchairs while the rest remain standing at the back and suffer from the heat, in spite of the air-conditioning. A screen, a platform, and the briefing is opened by the representa-tive of the civil press mission, Jack Stuart.

Short, round, white-haired, shoe-button eyes behind spectacles he likes to fiddle with, speaking between his teeth and spraying his audience three yards away, he finds it impossible to pronounce foreign names correctly, especially Vietnamese.

After listing the number of attacks that day, he announces the inevitable visit of this or that retired general or of some mission that happens to be in Vietnam on a study trip. Then comes the traditional 'No questions?'—and unless he is challenged by Joe Fried, Jack leaves the platform to the spokesmen for the Army, the Air Force, and the Navy: Lieut.-Col. Chase, Lieut.-Col. Rose, and Lieut.-Commander Lue Herzog.

Four maps representing the four army corps are projected on to the screen while detailed information is given on each paragraph of the press releases, duplicated copies of which each journalist has taken from special boxes at the entrance to the conference hall. These reports contain everything—or almost everything: Body count, K.I.A., killed in action; W.I.A., wounded in action; M.I.A.,

BH

8   WITH THE AMERICANS

missing in action; and the number of sorties made by fighter planes. For the B-52 raids, on a staff map which is also projected, a plane is drawn at the point of the objective.

On the map of North Vietnam the day's bombardments are marked in blue for the Air Force, black for the Navy. American casualty figures are rarely given in exact numbers, but with the qualification: heavy, medium or light losses.

'Do you have any more questions?'

That is when war begins, war between the officials and the journalists; a war known as the war of information. A verbal tilting-match that is in fact a game of cat and mouse.

If some journalists such as Peter Arnet, of Associated Press, or Tom Burkeley, of the *New York Times*, are among the 'moderates', others are quarrelsome by nature, and like silly young puppies, yap incessantly. Amongst those, the honours go without any doubt at all to Joe Fried, of the *New York Daily News*. Small, dark, unable to stay in one place for two minutes, he has become a mainstay of the briefings—first because he has been in Vietnam for three years, next because he hardly ever leaves Saigon. Though later on I got quite thrilled by the 'five o'clock follies', that first day I came away completely bewildered: my uncertain English, the special lingo, the code names that I'd have to learn if I wanted to follow this war and try to understand it. I seriously asked myself if I'd ever be able to cope with military affairs.

Then, after the press agencies have sent off their reports, comes the ritual tea on the terrace of the Continental Hotel. The latest news is discussed with passion and humour—often sick humour.

Snatches of conversation:

'I was with the Koreans. Real killers!'

'I'm fed up with the war! Four days march in the jungle! Impossible to get out of it! Not a shot! Not a picture! Nothing!'

'I'm leaving tomorrow with the 2nd of the 5th of the 101st!'

Not being in the know I felt like an intruder at a show, a show I hadn't been admitted to—not yet!

My housing problem settled—a flat in the rue Tu Do that IBM were not using—I decided to get going, too. But where? I had no idea.

The first step was equipment. All American goods can be found on the black market, spread out over the pavements of three or four

streets in the centre of town, on the ground or on trestles, piled on
top of each other, or arranged in boxes.

'What we can't get any longer at the P.X.,' the Americans told
me, 'we can pick up in the street.'

A bunch of American senators had been deeply stirred the year
before by these Saigonese 'flea markets'—they were touring Vietnam
to see how the taxpayers' money was being spent!

The scandal blows up every six months. After a violent press
campaign, the police ban, hunt and burn a selection of goods. These
are piled into great bonfires, to the huge delight of both kids and
cameramen.

But a few days later the market pops up again a few streets
farther off, cautiously at first, then a little more brazenly. Battle-
dress, T-shirts, belts, flasks, knapsacks, hammocks, ponchos, shoes,
military jungle boots with steel soles—all of them American by
origin.

There and nowhere else can the ordinary soldier buy the gear he
needs to follow his section into the field.

If what you want's not there—a short pause, a lot of whispering
and the stallholder vanishes, to reappear ten minutes later with the
size you asked for.

Where did he go for his stock?

Bargaining is a must. Are you French? The price comes down.
As with taxis and pedicabs, I'm beginning to realize that there are
three prices in Saigon—for the Americans, the French and the
Vietnamese.

Are they based on standard of living? On popularity? Or both?

Since none of the French journalists were going to the front for
the moment, I stayed for a while in Saigon.

For my first operation I wanted to follow a veteran. I was just
being practical. I didn't kid myself it would be enough to say, 'I'm
going to film the war.'

There must be procedures to follow, rules to keep, and I knew
neither one nor the other.

I listened to the Armed Forces Radio which begins its transmission
with a hearty 'Good morning, Vietnam!' followed by half an hour of
canned physical jerks.

I read the papers, three in English, two in French. As for Vietnamese dailies, there are thirty-five of them! It was the first time I'd

seen blank spaces—often half a column—on the front page of a newspaper.

Censorship is strict, quite openly enforced, and follows rules which seem incomprehensible to an outsider like myself. A speech made by Ky at Pleiku has been cut: three or four phrases struck out. But who by? And why? The text continues a few lines further down!

Manœuvres and attacks are naturally reported—with a forty-eight hour delay in the case of the French press.

On page three it is announced that such-and-such a pianist, or perhaps a lecturer, will perform that evening. There might even be a German travelling circus on tour for two weeks.

Camera in hand, I explore Saigon. In a pedicab, under a blazing sun, or alternatively in torrents of rain. It is the monsoon.

As the schools come out, the children splash ecstatically in water up to their thighs.

Saigon! What has not been said and written about this ancient Paris of South-East Asia, which has now become the sink of South Vietnam.

Saigon, which was planned originally for 500,000 inhabitants, numbers at this moment (including Cholon) 3 million. Now ten people are crammed together where there is scarcely room for five, shanty towns spring up, and children wander in the street, sleeping where they can, on the ground, on the pavements, under the porch of the Alliance Française.

No, I didn't see gallows erected in the market place. No, rubbish wasn't scattered all over the city. But what was true yesterday is not necessarily true today.

Apart from the crazy traffic that you can't ignore—my pedicab gave me cold sweats at every corner—the thing that struck me most at first was not the bars, but the children.

They are everywhere, hunting you down, hanging round hotels, markets, bars, in the streets, even where you least expect them. Impossible to take a step without seeing their outstretched hands.

'Give me five piastres or buy me this.'

They are organized in gangs. I got mixed up with three bloody street fights. This system of gangs has its own rules, which protect the members, but stop them from cheating the clan or leaving it, to desert to a rival group.

Without families, either because they no longer have one, or

because they themselves have left a home with too many mouths
to feed, with no fixed place to sleep, these urchins from the age of
seven or eight have already learnt to shift for themselves in the
asphalt jungle.

They cluster round the GIs offering them their sister, who is
'Number One'. But even as they hold out a hand, and get tangled
up in their legs, with a great burst of laughter they pull the down
from the arms of these hairy giants!

If the girls dream of having round eyes and a bust like Jayne
Mansfield, the smooth-faced boys are obsessed by razors that are
no use to them.

I remember reading in an article there: 'After a whole generation
of contact with the French, their diet has been enriched by all
kinds of products, with more and more varieties of vitamins, so their
figures are fuller, there's flesh on their bones.'

'Like hell!' was Fatty's comment. 'If that journalist believes in
the value of vitamins, he must have been here with his wife! He was
obviously in no position to verify his claims. But go and look in the
market! You'll find bras padded with sponge or inflated rubber,
openly displayed and selling in thousands.'

If these explain the change in silhouette of the Vietnamese girl
from the French to the American period (now she wants to look like
a *Playboy* pin-up) they also explain the G.I.s' disillusionment.

Ten centimetres more on the bust can be bought in the market-
place. But round eyes are more difficult to come by. At least you
must have money and be able to leave Vietnam, like Madame Ky—
for like her you must go to Japan for an operation.

Too bad if your husband bawls you out when you get back!

The bottom of the rue Tu Do and round about is the beat of
the famous 'Saigon Tea' girls, with their short, tight skirts, their
clinging sweaters, their bold make-up. A few of them, though,
keep their traditional tunics to make themselves more exotic in
local plumage.

The particular sort of snobbery amongst these girls, these
'hostesses' who earn as much as a commandant in the Vietnamese
army, or an important civil servant—his official salary, I mean, not
counting the under-the-counter dealings which go with his post—is
not to sleep with their clients, or at least not to make it a general
rule. They simply flirt with them over two glasses of tea, priced as

high as the most expensive whisky, and wait for eleven-thirty, the hour when such places close, before the midnight curfew.

As the night-clubs come out, there are dozens of pedicabs, of Vietnamese perched on backfiring Hondas, waiting for the G.I.s. The very broad range of the wares they offer—described always as 'Super Number One'—corresponds exactly to the demand.

'Number One' or 'Number Ten'! There is never anything between. This indicates at once that she is beautiful or ugly, good or absolutely disgusting, charming or an utter bitch. In the latter case she becomes Number Ten Thousand! But the interpretations can be varied to infinity.

In fact, what astonished me were not these bars with flashy girls, with glaring neon lights, which are called New York, Florida, Miami, Las Vegas or Cowboy, but the others, places like Maxim's, for example, where I met only Vietnamese, bloated and puffing cigars, their Mercedes at the door, war profiteers or government officials, and often both at once. Those places, a little smarter, are too expensive for the Americans!

For press correspondents, too! I was sorry about that, for the orchestra was excellent—a young pop group with long hair!

Going towards the port, on the other side of the bridge, is Harlem.

While at the front, in action, black and white fight side by side, in the camps and still more off duty segregation appears again. Quite naturally and with the tacit consent of both sides.

In Saigon the bars and the girls for the white-skinned G.I. are not the same as those for his dark-skinned brother. Nor are the prices—Vietnamese prostitution is race-conscious.

In Saigon there are also 35,000 Americans that the High Command would like to group all together in a camp outside the city. In the meantime, they are divided between the base at Tan Son Nhut, and various hotels and barred buildings—bars which don't stop them being attacked—and guarded by M.P.s, who are in turn surrounded and protected by sand-bags.

Propaganda credits them with being tough, their finger always on the trigger. I find them more human than that, relaxed and joking, chatting to girls and to children. Too trusting, in fact.

As for the Vietnamese M.P.s, though they're armed with machine-guns, their casual attitude cancels out their threatening appearance.

These fragile-looking buildings with paper-thin partitions spring up like mushrooms, the demand being always greater than the supply, in spite of the exorbitant rents. But as I was taking shots of them, it was not their number that surprised me in those early days, but the labourers working on them—all women.

In the streets it is also women who clear away the rubbish, dig up the roads and lay them again. As there is always work in progress in the centre of the town, they gather during their lunch break in the square of rue Tu Do, or in the gardens behind the Sports Club. In these gardens, as in gardens everywhere, lovers walk hand in hand, and sit on the benches gazing at each other, with eyes for no one else.

The Sports Club is the society meeting-place for the 'crème de la crème', the smart set of Saigon: French, American and Vietnamese.

Tennis courts, bridge rooms, a restaurant on the edge of the swimming pool, and everything laid on for sunbathing, where you can lie flat on your back, squinting your eyes against the sun which blinds them, trying to pick out the Phantoms or the F.100s which pass overhead and stop you sleeping.

If the French moan about their club being invaded by Colonels or diplomats from the American Embassy, the Americans are irritated at having to apply for membership to a committee entirely composed of Frenchmen—these 'colonials' who profit by their presence, and yet criticize them openly. Both here and at the Givral, which is the bar of the French shopkeepers where the best cakes in town can be found, the comments are the same, and so are the smiles of satisfaction.

'You saw about the beating they took yesterday?'

'An F.100 shot down at the gates of Saigon!'

'Tan Son Nhut has been attacked again!'

'Nine killed yesterday in a brawl at a G.I. bar!'

'If we had only had a quarter of their resources!'

In fact, perhaps unconsciously, the French are jealous, rather than actively anti-American. They are bitter, too.

'If only they'd helped us before. . . .'

Indo-China, which they loved and lost, now belongs to 'the others', who have everything and, who knows, might even win the war. A thought that certainly gives the Frenchman a pang.

But their wounded vanity is soothed by the affection of the Vietnamese who tell them:

'We have much more in common with you. . . .'

And because that is true, the gap that separates the 'imperialistic' Americans from the 'colonial' French has widened.

Though English is now the ruling language, Ky's speeches are always written in French before being translated. For didn't he study at the Meknes Flying school at the time when Morocco was still French?

The height of snobbery amongst officials or Vietnamese officers is to speak French at cocktail parties, leaving the Americans to stumble over the grammatical rules or to chew on their grievances alone in a corner.

None of which prevents the Vietnamese from demonstrating in front of the French Embassy, closed since the diplomatic rupture, in protest against the French schools. Even though the news rates five columns in the local press against one in Paris, it is actually less serious seen close at hand. The demonstrators take a much less determined attitude than the communiqués would lead you to believe. Perhaps they were not paid well enough.

The only people who try to stay outside these national quarrels are the Corsicans.

They realize: 'As long as there are Americans, there'll be money!'

All the 'with-it' restaurants are run by Corsicans—from the Dolce Vita to the Aterbea, with the Admiral and the Cave in between. Dominique, who guards his accent carefully, is the uncrowned king of this Corsican coterie, who were already a group by the time of the first Indo-Chinese war.

Corsican men and Vietnamese women are in the strongest position as proprietors of bars and other places of that kind. Sometimes, in the background, there are a few American colonels, who make their money work for them this way.

While French cuisine is very widespread, it is by contrast very difficult to eat Vietnamese food in Saigon or Cholon. All the exotic restaurants are Chinese. Of course, in the town, there are little stalls selling local dishes. But for the marvellous *crabes au sel*, the *cha gio* or the *bœuf marmite* you must go to the Binh Loi bridge.

Four kilometres from the town, it's the favourite spot to take the 'tourist' journalist, on his forty-eight hour visit. The two restaurants, built on stilts, are out of bounds for American troops. There we French and the Vietnamese are on our own.

Every night there are goings-on in the immediate neighbourhood of the two 'straw-hut' restaurants where the guests often have to crouch under the tables when the swapping of bullets becomes too enthusiastic. Open-mouthed, the visiting foreigner watches soldiers darting from bush to bush two yards away from him, their fingers on the trigger of an M16. With a bit of luck, a journalist too anxious to get away might get mixed up in the action. His paper will be only too glad of it. And there have never been any actual deaths at Binh Loi.

Strange town, full of contrasts—the G.I.s aren't allowed to go to Binh Loi, but, on the other hand, they don't hesitate to plunge alone into the dark streets of Cholon, the Chinese quarter, looking for girls in this maze of nameless blind alleys, where it would be only too easy to disappear without a trace.

And what about those queues of officers lined up along the pavement, in the thick of the traffic and reading the morning paper while they wait for a bus with bars to take them to their offices—also barred? Anyone at all could hurl a grenade at them, without being spotted. In point of fact that happens from time to time, but very rarely.

On Sundays some of these officers leave the shelter of their guarded hotels, and take a flip between Tan Son Nhut and Bien Hoa, which is where the jets land.

Others go by boat or car to the Yacht Club a few kilometres down the river. On the right bank the French club, on the other side the American club. So each one sticks to his own group, and asks for nothing better. In both places there are well-kept lawns and flowers, and a swimming pool.

As in Paris, London or New York, it's a bore coming home on Sunday evening, with the roads crowded, and traffic jams. The Vietnamese, too, have been out to get some fresh air, bathing at Cap Saint-Jacques, fishing in the river, or strolling towards Bien Hoa.

Or again, like the driver of my pedicab, perhaps they've spent their afternoon at the races. Oh, yes! Gambling exists at Saigon, like anywhere else, and the Vietnamese are great gamblers! At the beginning of the autoroute, there are public television sets installed in the street six feet above the ground.

Next to the race course there is a golf course; next to the golf course, a riding school and a show-ring.

And that's how you can spend your Sundays in Saigon!

'I can't work after six o'clock today, madame,' my driver told me, 'I'm going to a boxing-match.'

I went with him. We had to elbow our way in. The stadium was packed. My height was an advantage, I was a good head taller than anyone else. There were four fights, and one of them . . . for women! Between each bout, an interval, with music, pop groups, singers; the boys had long hair and the girls mini-skirts.

'The police don't like long hair,' said my guide. 'It's illegal now. They must cut it. Or else, it's prison.'

As we came out, a '4CV' exploded a hundred yards away from us, and reminded me that the Vietcong, too, amuse themselves on Sundays. Vietnamese police, American M.P.s, white truncheons, piercing whistles. I had to show my press card to keep my driver from being arrested. There was a roundup, and everybody was carted off for an identity check, for questioning.

When it all calmed down, I went home on foot. Nearly three kilometres. No one in the streets. It was curfew-time. I felt that Saigon belonged to me. But no—Saigon belongs at night, in fact, to the police patrols, to the M.P.s. In armoured cars, bristling with guns, they are on the lookout for Vietcong commandos or for drunken G.I. stragglers.

'Papers, please.'

I replied in French. They apologized, and radioed for a car of Vietnamese police, the only ones—in theory—who have the right to check civilian papers. Sometimes problems arise. The M.P.s once arrested and carted off the Prefect of Saigon! American soldiers dared to ask a civilian for his papers. . . . And to arrest him! An official! Fair enough—but that official had been signalling on the port, armed with an automatic rifle!

In Saigon there are also streets barricaded by coils of barbed wire. And in Hai Bai Trung, the main road that links the harbour to Tan Son Nhut or Bien Hoa, is a long unbroken line of brand-new tanks and newly-arrived cannons. To wind up the night's procession, well guarded and protected at every cross-roads, planes just unloaded from giant air freighters from San Francisco crawled forward, wings folded, under the light of powerful arc-lamps that lit up the whole avenue. An incongruous sight in the streets of a city dead now and for a few more hours under the curfew!

2

The War

War!—I never imagined it would be like this. I pictured to myself a series of engagements and pitched battles. I'd been marching with the Marines for four days and still nothing. Except the heat and the mosquitoes, clothing sticking to our skin, sweat running into our eyes, knapsacks quickly becoming too heavy with the straps cutting into our shoulders, and water-bottles emptying too quickly. Those boots I'd thought so marvellous at the black market in Saigon now seemed to weigh a ton. And that camera which was giving me blisters on my hands.

To film what? Who? G.I.s marching, who never stop marching—feet, always feet! Or eating their C-rations, sitting down with legs folded under them and forearms resting on their knees.

For my first operation I'd hoped for a colleague, preferably a Frenchman because of my shaky English. After all, it was the first time I'd gone to war. I was afraid of not understanding, of not knowing how to behave, of making a fool of myself.

One afternoon in the A.F.P. office in Saigon I met a childhood friend, Christian Simonpiétri. We were in the same class in Nice. Now a photographer, he'd been in Vietnam for three years. Until the previous March his wife and daughter had been with him. They lived in Da Nang. Then came the Buddhists' revolt: 'I just had time to get Michou and the child away. The house was looted and turned upside down.'

'By the Buddhists?'

'Good heavens, no! By Government troops. My family have gone back to France. I'm going to join them soon.'

Meanwhile, here he was. He taught me how to dig my fox-hole for the night.

'Even if you're dead tired and have only one wish, to lie down—dig! The mortars come quickly, and the shells fall anywhere!'

We tried to make a tent out of our rainproof ponchos. But as he was no more a handyman than I am, a sergeant came to our rescue. During the day I longed for cool, fresh air. At night, rolled up in a ball in my hole, my teeth chattered with the cold.

I jumped when the artillery began to pound. Theirs or ours? I didn't know. I risked a quick look round. Good, it's all right! They weren't Vietcong mortars, for all was quiet, no one stirred.

As long as they behave like men, while remaining quite feminine— quite a difficult pose to maintain—female journalists are accepted in action.

My toilet things were limited to a toothbrush and some toothpaste in the left pocket of my jacket; soap, a pair of tweezers, and a mirror in the right. My helmet served as a washbasin and a bathtub at the same time!

On the second day I found a solution to my most pressing problem: by forcing myself to drink moderately I only needed privacy in the evening, when darkness came, or in the early morning at dawn!

From time to time, gun shots. Then nothing more. We'd begin to march again.

War involves waiting more than anything, an endless patience. Waiting for plane, for helicopter, for contact with the enemy.

'And when you make contact,' a G.I. told me, 'you wait for it to stop! You're always waiting. But most of all, you wait for the end of the war.'

'When I die, I'll go to heaven, for I've been through hell in Vietnam.' The Marines have written this sentence everywhere: on lighters, on key-rings; even tattooed on their arms.

'Do you earn a lot of money for doing this job and taking so many risks?' the G.I.s asked me.

In those early days, I told the truth.

'I'm making a documentary film which might not even be shown. But the problem of this war fascinates me: that's a good enough reason.'

After I'd had more experience, I simply said, 'Yes, lots of money!'

They were proud of me. They were reassured. They understood me. All of them—G.I.s, as well as officers, approached me, 'What do you think of de Gaulle?'

I was not all that keen to talk politics on the march, and breathless. So I told them, 'Well, you know, not everyone in France loves him.'

Which was the last thing I should have said!

'Ah! But you're wrong! All Frenchmen must be proud of him.' And they would add: 'But why doesn't he like us?'

They were surprised—and sad! De Gaulle makes them ask such questions.

We had now left the plain for the mountain, and the forest was growing more dense. Still some isolated snipers, but nothing to be seen. And we had no idea what was happening. The radio announced that there were two or three casualties a little farther on. Alpha Company had been under mortar fire, and the helicopters could not land. So they quickly cleared a corner of the forest, cut down two or three trees, so that the little rescue baskets could be lowered to haul up the wounded.

But all that was happening too far away. I was following operations thanks to the field radio station that transmitted conversation like the sound-track of a film without the picture. To photograph war, you must be up to your neck in it. And it all goes too fast. In a few minutes the skirmish is over. Or else there is a real battle. Then like Fabrice at Waterloo, you have no idea what's happening, stuck in a hole or behind a tree with three soldiers or at the most, four, in your field of vision.

I saw my first dead body in the Delta during another operation. We were advancing in line through a paddy field with water up to our chests. I was with a battalion of Vietnamese Rangers. We were hunting for a Vietcong prison camp which spies had located near Ben Tre in the mouth of the Mekong.

The 'Viets' had begun to fire on us the moment we jumped from the helicopters. We had to run for it immediately, or rather try to run, for we were wading in the water. The bullets sent up little waterspouts all along the line of soldiers. And then suddenly one of the men fell forward and lay flat on the bank, without a sound. I thought at first he'd lost his footing. I wanted to help him get up. But the American adviser with the company, who was just behind me, gave me a shove in the back and said, 'Go ahead! He's dead!'

In the end we found the camp but the prisoners had disappeared. The noise of the helicopters was enough to warn them. Moreover, we had lost time. It seemed to me that we'd been going round in circles.

'You're quite right,' admitted the American captain, 'We've already passed this point three times.'

I went along on five or six operations led by Vietnamese troops in the Delta, with the 7th, 9th and 21st Divisions, either in the field or at the forward command post. It was always the same thing. The Vietnamese captain—or *day-uy*—would show me one position, while the American adviser would give me another.

At the command post on a huge staff map, there were always two colours: one for the position of the company announced by the Vietnamese radio, the other by the American radio. The observation plane gave the exact point—and it was always the American who was right. Luckily, the 'spy' plane was there! Otherwise, we would have been bombed every time by the U.S. Air Force—which happens even so, occasionally.

Before attacking territory south of the 17th Parallel, air headquarters must have permission from the head of the Vietnam province. The operation is then directed by a reconnaissance plane, which watches and controls each run, counting the number of hits. If the weather is bad, the plane is replaced by radar, which then guides the jets.

Sometimes there are 'errors', and civilians are killed. It's also happened that an American section has been 'napalmed'.

In the summer of 1966 when I had already arrived in Vietnam, a hamlet near the village of Truong Trung was bombed. The American command announced:

'Twenty-four villagers killed and eighty-two wounded. Almost all were women and children.'

But the official spokesman replied 'Yes' to three questions put to him by the journalists:

'Were there any Vietcong in the hamlet during the attack? Had the inhabitants been forced to stay there in spite of the bombing? Did the Vietcong shoot down the reconnaissance plane in charge of the operation?' In psychological warfare there must be martyrs. Tito made this very clear in his account of the Yugoslav Resistance.

In the Delta, towards Soctrang, I passed through an area that had just been bombed and 'napalmed'. It was not even a village, just a few huts scattered among the palm trees. From a distance of two kilometres, I had seen the planes dive and drop their loads. And now we were there. The houses had stopped burning, but the stench was unbearable. Just a few women and children, squatting on their heels. During the attack, they had stayed in the shelters round the houses. They watched us pass without seeing us, they were far away. Their eyes were dead.

Two months later, when I was under American bombing myself after my capture by the Vietcong, I came to understand how they survived.

I don't think I shall ever be able to film a dead man. Still less a wounded one. To circle round him, pointing my camera at him, would be impossible for me. And yet such pictures are necessary to show the full horror of war.

To hear young boys screaming with pain as they waited to be rescued, made me sick. Helicopters always came to evacuate them, even in the thick of the fighting. The G.I. knows they'll come. He knows that he won't be left behind. That gives him the confidence to fight.

At the military field hospital in Hammond, the doctor told me, 'We save ninety-eight per cent of those who get here alive.'

During Operation Attleboro I saw the bodies of dead American soldiers picked up. After their identification discs had been forced between their teeth, they were put into huge plastic bags with zips. Then they were sent to the morgue at Tan Son Nhut, and from there taken back by plane to the United States.

I had seen part of that First Division disembark at Vang Tau, the old Cap Saint-Jacques of the French, a few days after my arrival. After forty-five days at sea the infantrymen had solid earth beneath their feet again. The landing craft ran gently aground on the sandy beach, lowering their steel bows to let the soldiers out. The first soldier, from the leading boat, carried a star-spangled banner in his hand.

'We are here to defend freedom!' the officer beside the flag-bearer declaimed. A military band was waiting for them. Graceful young Vietnamese girls draped wreaths of flowers round their necks, kissed them, thanked them for coming! This simple ceremony was some-how very touching. And I was not the only one with tears in my eyes. I knew, all the same, that it was only an act, that wreaths of flowers are not a Vietnamese custom, but an American one imported from Hawaii.

Perhaps some of those soldiers were among the dead of Attleboro. But there were no flowers for them now, no music. Only the mud of the rice fields. And perhaps, too, in the last spasm of death, fear and one question . . . Why?

3

Sailors are Superstitious

'Do you still want to go in an aircraft carrier?' Commander Jack MacKircher, press officer of the Seventh Fleet at Saigon, asked me one day.

Two months before, the same Commander had told me, 'I'm terribly sorry. Women are not allowed to sleep on board. Sailors are superstitious.'

No doubt Jack had changed his mind when faced with an influx of women journalists to Vietnam.

If, at the 'five o'clock follies', long hair was more and more common, while the scent of perfume or make-up mingled with cigarettes, it was the plaits—'pigtails' as the Americans call them—that won the honours of the battlefield. There were a dozen of us. In fact, thirteen! An unlucky number! All Americans, except for Cathy and me. Among the Americans, Denby Fawcett was the most popular. Blonde, twenty-five years old, once a surfing champion, she was the correspondent for a Honolulu daily. She arrived originally with her fiancé, also a reporter, but when he left, Denby stayed on to work and to carry her smile and her frankness all over Vietnam.

'When Denby or Michèle are in our group,' said John Bethelsem of *Newsweek*, 'there are no more transport or priority problems. They get whatever they want, including the special helicopter!'

As for J. Hardy, though she hasn't been captured by the Vietcong, she has been by a journalist, press chief at U.S.A.I.D.—he has just made her his wife!

Not all women journalists went to the front. Usually they were happy to stay at the press centres or at H.Q.—in the company of so-called 'masculine' colleagues. However, it was not a man, but a woman photographer who held the record for the number of operations undertaken—and by a good length. A Frenchwoman! Naturally! The youngest of us all, at that—twenty-two years old,

CH

and knee-high to a grasshopper. She was nick-named Hedge-Hopper. Her shortness—only four feet eleven—no doubt made it easier for her to dodge the bullets, like Gregory in the song of Botrel.

The Marines had just begun to forgive Cathy Leroy her men's talk and her very choice language when she consigned to all the devils the helicopter pilot who didn't want to take her aboard, and the other correspondents were also thrown off because of her.

She was wounded photographing the biggest battle of Vietnam, Hill 881, the battle that got the greatest amount of trans-Atlantic publicity. Johnson must have been trying to impress on his fellow itizens that their beloved Marines had need of reinforcements. And that everyone must support the demand for another 70,000 men before the end of the year, to reach the goal of half a million. The 'leathernecks' made Cathy an honorary member of the Marine Corps. But I don't think—at least it's not like them—that it was because of their love of publicity. She had shared their difficulties, their sufferings. She was now one of them.

In the company of three other journalists, I left Da Nang—under a blazing sun—aboard a twin-engined plane that was to take us to the Gulf of Tonkin, to look for the *Coral Sea*, somewhere north of the 17th Parallel.

With my back to the pilot, an axe in my hand, a double safety belt—an extra one around my shoulders—wedged into a canary-yellow Mae West, with anti-shark powder and a signal light, I found it difficult to move.

But when the pilot cried, 'There she is!' and began extricating himself from his gear, we all craned forward to try to catch a glimpse in the vast infinity of the China Sea, where the blue of the water and the sky were indistinguishable, of something which seemed to be no bigger than a nutshell.

A tiny boat that quickly became a monster, a mastodon of steel with a belly full of bombs. Electronic machines obeyed by 3,800 human robots. A monster which, twenty-four hours out of twenty-four, steams on at forty kilometres an hour.

Blinded by the sun, already deafened by the roar of the jets, choking from the smell of burning oil, we were welcomed by a positive battalion of press officers, white caps in one hand, the other extended for a hearty 'Welcome aboard the U.S.S. *Coral Sea*!'

After a lecture, with slides showing the lay-out of the ship, each of us had a guide to go ahead of us and give us our bearings, to explain things to us, and take us to all the levels of this floating city. The press service was well organized. Almost every question had been anticipated and the answer was to be found in the press-kit we had been handed when we first came aboard.

On the first page, circled in red, were nine security instructions: No smoking, of course; but also no hats to be worn (a hat caught in the jets can cost lives and involve *great expense*); keep clear of restricted areas, which include radar installations and the Combat Information Centre; don't touch any switches or control buttons (the life of the ship may depend on them); call 204 if you see even the smallest suspicious flame; or 999 if you are ill; finally, be careful of companionways and ladders, dangerous for the uninitiated, and specially at night, of all the ropes and boat hooks and hawsers which lie about the deck.

Then began an exhausting tour. We went up, and down, turned right, then left, down again, then up again, up almost vertical steps. A labyrinth where, in spite of the notices, it was easy to get lost. I felt really lost in this maze of streets and alley-ways and cat-walks, spread out over seven different levels in which every inter-section has either its soda-fountain or an ice-cream dispenser.

Among the facilities were a printing press (turning out a monthly magazine and a daily paper), post office, cinema, shoemaker, barbers (one for the officers, another for the men), dry-cleaners, laundry, tailor, Turkish baths, photographic lab., and a P.X. An operating theatre and a dental surgery have also been installed, somewhere in the heart of the monster.

But the *Coral Sea* is primarily a collection of statistics and com-parisons: 63,000 tons of steel; 973 feet long, the equivalent of three football fields; as tall as a twenty-storey building; 2,500 rooms. More than 2,000 electric motors. The amount of oil burnt in her would heat 3,000 houses for a year, and the salary of those 3,800 officers and men amounts to more than 500,000 dollars—the monthly turnover of the different shops being 35,000 dollars. Her evaporators are capable of producing more than 1,200,000 litres of drinking water. Fourteen thousand cups of coffee can be prepared at the same time, and the kitchens serve more than 10,000 meals a day.

As for her engine power, it equals the strength of 140 locomotives, and her production in kilowatt hours could supply electricity for a city of a million inhabitants.

Below decks, in huge hangers, sleep the seventy-five planes —bombers, fighters and others—which are carried by the *Coral Sea*.

All these figures whirled round in my head. Everything I had just seen existed to serve those 'birds' with shark-noses and folded wings of silver, waiting for another mission, a mission of death and destruction, each plane capable of stowing in its flanks between 3,000 and 4,000 pounds of bombs. From the Phantom to the Skywarrior, by way of the Crusader and the Skyhawk, they were all there.

On every side bombs were neatly stacked in bays—bombs of every size and description, classified and numbered, awaiting their turn.

From the height of the bridge, where Captain Frank W. Ault received me, I had a grandstand view of the dance of death, the carousel of the 'jets', set in motion by officers pressing buttons.

The press-kit stated: 'To the casual observer operations from the flight-deck give an impression of complete chaos; but in fact those operations are among the best drilled and most complex on board the *Coral Sea*.'

Men in green, red, blue, maroon or yellow overalls, crash helmets on their heads and huge earplugs in their ears, dashed about, running—it seemed to me—in all directions. Some gave automatic, robot-like signals, and others shoved trolleys around in the midst of the jets, which took off with an infernal roar as others surged up from the darkness, mounted on lifts.

Each group of seven or eight men wore a particular colour to indicate the nature of their job between take-off and landing: three planes leave every minute for a period of twenty minutes, then a pause of fifteen minutes to prepare the three runways for the return manœuvre, and to finish loading the bombs.

Three monsters growled and spat, still reined in by the catapults, before breaking loose with apocalyptic fury. The whole ship shuddered, racked by the vibration.

Jammed between two trolleys, my camera balanced on a bomb, it was quite impossible to hold it still. Waves of heat from the jet engines blurred the white lines in the view-finder. And each time the electric catapults unleashed another rearing, roaring thunderbolt, all the men in coloured overalls were enveloped in a white cloud which made them seem unreal. And this grind goes on and on, for twelve hours out of twenty-four. From midday to midnight. During the pauses, the ground-crew sailors slump, stretched out on a trolley, with a bomb or a rocket for a pillow.

I was not the only person filming. Television cameras, scattered all over the deck, recorded each landing, each take-off. These pictures are reproduced on strategically-placed screens throughout the aircraft carrier. It is a 'spy system', trying to discover and pin-point the smallest technical fault, or the slightest negligence.

As he returns from his mission, each pilot, with his flying gear still on his back and his face still streaked with sweat, must go straight to his squadron's conference room, to see the film of his take-off and landing.

What does Vietnam mean to these men?

Women? Children? Slant-eyed men in black pyjamas? Sun or paddy fields or soup at street corners? Children, burnt by napalm, and evacuated to hospitals? The long, dreary marches in search of an enemy who eludes them? Or at the end, the brutal, bloody contact? The bodies of comrades torn to shreds by a grenade, or impaled on the iron teeth of a trap? Heat and sweat? And back in camp, exhausted, still the fear of an attack? Nights in the shelters under Vietcong mortar fire? A population that might be friend or foe?

No. All that means nothing to them.

For these pilots Vietnam is nothing more than a map, with targets, objectives to be co-ordinated, buttons to be pressed, a dogfight with the Migs, or 'lousy' weather which will give them zero visibility, mess up their mission, and force them to drop their tons of explosive somewhere in the China Sea. Sometimes it also means rescuing one of their number from that vast expanse of blue, or from that green mass—the jungle.

But though they know the jungle from above, they know nothing about it from below. One by one the pilots asked me elementary questions about politics, about Ky, about the country, about the way in which the war on the ground is being fought. I was supposed to be asking the questions, and they ended by interviewing me.

Exceptional cases apart, the pilots are not granted leave in Vietnam.

Two months before some Marines, near the demilitarized zone, had told me,

'For a week we had two Navy pilots here. They wanted to see at first hand what they had been bombing for more than six months.'

But that is rare. And what those pilots thought when they returned to their air-conditioned world I do not know.

In the Combat Information Centre each squadron, composed usually of four jets and an observation plane, a Skyraider, studies and receives the most detailed instructions about the next mission. Each operation takes at least four hours of preparation, the chief concern being to avoid civilian losses.

With a special permit, I was able to get into that briefing room where, on the huge map of North Vietnam, were planted flags of different colours showing objectives already gained, and still to be tackled—further steps on the ladder to victory. A map of China was there, too, in the background.

After a rest and a 'supervitamized' meal, the pilot in his specially camouflaged overalls with dozens of pockets where, if he needs it, he'll find a mirror essential for signalling his pals to come and help him, and a dictionary of a hundred or so Vietnamese words, goes to chapel. This man who is leaving for the skies above Vietnam, with the same objective as the day before, or even the day before that— a section of road, perhaps, that has already been repaired by the 'ants' in two or three hours—has begun to have complexes.

February 7, 1965, the first day of the attack, is long past. It was possible to hope then that the North Vietnamese would surrender. But in spite of the tons of steel, of flame and iron, that the planes have constantly poured down on them, these stubborn Tonkinese are still holding out.

Yet the pilot knows that he belongs to the most powerful air force in the world. He knows that it would take less than twenty-four hours—even without atomic weapons—to annihilate North Vietnam. Nevertheless, the enemy still snaps his fingers at them, and in spite of the heaviest poundings still passes along this road— the pilot's principal objective—hundreds, even thousands of men (7,000 a month) who travel by convoy as far as the 17th Parallel, and from there infiltrate into the south.

Washington says: 'If it were not for these bombings, the infiltration would be even greater.'

So at each new stage of the air war the pilot makes his 'crate' rear up impatiently like a restless mare to stifle the doubts that are beginning to creep over him, and sits in the cockpit convincing himself till his eyes are shining again:

'The target is different today!'

It was the first time a woman had slept aboard the *Coral Sea*, but a *powder room* had been provided.

Captain Wault gave me his cabin, with an armed guard at the door. He himself slept on the bridge, where he had another cabin.

The sailors honoured me with a huge cake:

WELCOME MICHÈLE

With an interview thrown in and of course the inevitable question: 'How do you feel being the only woman on board tonight, with more than 3,800 men who haven't seen a girl for three months?'

During dinner, I told the story about Tim Page, the English photographer who was wounded three times: the first time by the Vietcong during an operation; the second time at Da Nang by the Buddhists during their demonstrations; and the third by the U.S. Air Force, which had mistaken an American patrol-boat for a North Vietnamese battleship.

'Yes,' the Vice-Admiral replied, laughing, 'three enemies!'

After the cinema show—a different film each night—at ten o'clock, I had a great surprise. On to the television screens, flashed a programme entitled *An Hour with Michèle*! I don't know whether the television cameras had conscientiously recorded all the landings and take-offs that day, but one thing is certain—they had filmed me from a distance, and in close-up, in the process of talking, of interviewing, of taking photographs, with or without my helmet—non-stop and everywhere, Michèle for one whole hour!

This programme was broadcast to the ships escorting the *Coral Sea*—the cruisers, the destroyers, the supply ships! Part of that Seventh Fleet where all comes down to numbers: 125 ships, 650 planes and 64,000 officers and ratings!

And, though the *Coral Sea* never slackened speed, towards five o'clock in the morning the supply ship managed to come alongside. The loading was done with gaff hooks, pulleys, transfers of bigger and bigger baskets. Day dawned on this operation, which went on for two hours to the music of the *Coral Sea*'s band stationed on the deck. The giant of the seas was saying 'Thank you!'

After spending twenty-four hours on board, we left at noon with the first wave of jets. With my Mae West firmly buckled, my head pressed against the backrest, both safety belts fastened as tight as possible, I took one last look at the axe and the escape hatch. My throat was so tight I felt I was going to choke. Then came the catapulting, the send-off from the aircraft carrier, a unique experience! A brutal experience which, in spite of our harness, flung us, bent double, against the seat ahead. A plunge towards the sea as the plane left the runway before gaining altitude at the very moment when we were about to skim the foam of the waves. As I watched the *Coral Sea* vanishing on the horizon till it was only the smallest dot, names, numbers, and comparisons whirled about in my head.

The pilots' faces and shining eyes became blurred, and faded into pictures of those other pilots at Hanoi, emaciated, hollow-eyed and lost. From an air-conditioned, push-button world, they have been catapulted, without transition, into a reality which is not theirs, a reality which they do not understand.

4

Operation 'Michèle'

The motto of the Special Forces: *De oppresso liber!*

The Special Forces, the famous 'Green Berets'—Robin Moore has celebrated them in a book, and John Wayne has portrayed them on the screen. Mercenaries, professional soldiers they certainly are, incapable of leading a normal life apart from fighting, and yet a certain mystery, a certain aura surrounds them. I decided to go and see them in action, not in an ordinary camp, but on an island: the island of Phu Ghoc.

Captain Davis, the press officer attached to the IVth Army corps at Cantho, warned me, 'Colonel Kelly, the Commander-in-Chief of the Special Forces, based at Nha Trang, doesn't like reporters.'

'Because of the book about his Green Berets?'

'He doesn't want women in camp, specially near the front.'

I therefore resorted to devious methods, and went to see the head of the district. General Thi, in command of the South Vietnamese Seventh Division, and therefore of Phu Ghoc, would have to inform Colonel Kelly by radio. For two hours I waited at midday under a burning sun, sitting on one of the wheels of the single-engined plane which would have to take me to the island.

'You're going to Phu Ghoc? Things are pretty hot down there! A fortnight ago five Americans were caught in an ambush. The jungle? Crammed full of Vietcong and bloodsuckers!'

'I know.'

At my calm reply they shrugged their shoulders.

Green water, deep and clear, the islands. . . . They say that Ky intends to organize a skin-diving party on one of the islands and invite members of the diplomatic corps. White sand, miles of beach and coconut palms.

But also a camp of political prisoners right beside the landing strip. In spite of my numerous requests, I would not be allowed to visit it.

The moment I landed in the little village of Duong Dong I was choked by the smell: it wasn't possible to overlook the fact that Phi Ghoc produces the best nuoc-mâm* in all Vietnam.

The head man of the district was 'unfortunately' not at home—a trick I had anticipated:

'Only one thing for it: go up to the camp. You can't stay here alone,' Captain William Maple told me. 'The village is not safe, and we expect a Vietcong attack any night.'

'But what about Colonel Kelly?'

'Don't worry. Say it's a case of *force majeure*!'

That evening, 'Black Jack' (Kelly's code name) bellowed over the radio, 'Get her out of there on the next plane!'

'Yes, sir! But the next plane is in three days' time,' replied Sergeant Harman, the radio operator, giving me a wink.

Phu Ghoc, Special Forces Camp

High on a rocky promontory, and built on the same model as other camps that I visited afterwards, there were nine Americans to about 120 Vietnamese.

For everyone alike: wooden huts with corrugated iron roofs. The only difference: no mess for the Vietnamese, but a little kitchen in the corner of each hut.

The *day-uy*—captain in Vietnamese—buys his beer or Coca Cola from the Americans' cold store.

I got the impression that one of the exclusive features of a Special Forces Camp is the rats. They are everywhere. They come and go, completely at home.

Though the Americans are only 'advisers' with the South Vietnamese regular units, here they had in fact assumed command.

Vietnamese Special Forces are called *Luc Luong Dac Biet* or L.L.D.B. One interpretation of those intials, which shows the respect their 'advisers' have for them, is 'lousy little dirty bastards' I was there to try to check the truth of such expressions.

As an integral part of the regular army—A.R.V.N. (Army of the Republic of Vietnam)—the L.L.D.B. are entitled to a number of special advantages, in particular, better equipment which is supplied directly by their 'advisers'. The Green Berets are also

* *Nuoc-mâm*: juice of dried fish, with a very strong smell, which is a basic seasoning for all Vietnamese cooking.

responsible for forming special battalions. Their emblem is a death's-head.

They are part of the C.I.D.G.* programme and are paid directly by the Americans. These men—many are *Nungs*,† renowned for their courage and their loyalty—these 'bruisers', as they are called, sign up for six months to two years.

At Cantho, Major Chuan, head of the L.L.D.B., told me: 'Recruitment is very difficult, for we are not supposed to take men who have been called up for service.'

Vietnamese shock troops—there are three companies in the Delta, ten missions in the six preceding months. They specialize in raids and ambushes, and in strengthening camp defences.

I was not to see the special battalions in action. They had just left Phu Ghoc after a three weeks' stay during which they had run into two Vietcong ambushes in which five Americans had died.

As the result of those two bloody clashes, there had been a change of command. For several days the two captains were there together, one waiting to succeed the other. With two entirely different attitudes to the war, they watched each other, with no respect.

Amid bursts of mortar fire a swarm of Vietnamese girls swept, and washed and sorted linen. William Maple, still nominally in charge, shouted orders. Of Indian descent, born in El Paso, Texas, thirty-four years ago, Captain Maple was a square-jawed man with a sensuous mouth and an expression that was assured and condescending. He was thick-set, with crew cut hair, and he walked with a little swagger; the very prototype of the professional soldier who enjoyed his work to the full. He was all for a policy of constant harassment.

'In six months there won't be a single Vietcong left on this island. The infiltration through Cambodia will be stopped.'

In the middle of all this commotion, and these differences of opinion, I moved in. Between the office and the sleeping quarters. Two mats and a bed—my room! When I used the shower, a sign, 'Female only', was provided, plus a kindly sentry.

The first day, I went to Duong Dong to film, accompanied by

* C.I.D.G.: Civil Irregular Defense Group.
† *Nungs*: A Chinese tribe from the Tonkin frontier, subject to South Vietnam since the Geneva Accord. The French had already formed them into special battalions. At that time they nicknamed them 'umbrella handles'.

Tony the interpreter. He was twenty years old, bubbling over with enthusiasm for his new captain.

'He's a real professional. He loves war! In the field when we're all dead tired after four or five days' march, he's still on the go. And with that dynamic energy of his, he keeps us going, too. But see how quiet and peaceful it is here.'

We are entering a village. Women were mending fishing nets spread out at the water's edge, and boats, full of fish, were heading towards the shore.

Though the stench was sometimes nauseating, I liked those peaceful little fishing villages in which *nuoc-mâm* factories were lined up one after the other. We had Chinese soup followed by a game of billards at the local bar (which the Green Berets call 'Chez Lyndon Johnson') in the company of some old men who chewed tobacco, and the inevitable horde of kids.

Back at camp, Maple briefed his men and the Vietnamese officers on the new operation, which was to be launched the following evening:

'Forty-five men, four Green Berets, and I myself will make up team number one. A Navy boat will land us on the north end of the island, and we'll have to get across undergrowth, jungle and mountains. Group Number Two, commanded by the *day-uy* with Lieutenant Levin's help, will act as the 'blocking force'. That is, they will work their way up the island and rejoin us at point X.

'Once the two companies make contact, we'll come back to camp together. Estimated length of the operation: four days and four nights. Objective: to cross territory where there's never been any action. According to our information service, we should find a hospital and a cache of arms and ammunition. Enemy strength: impossible to calculate exactly, but certainly considerable. Remember—we'll risk running into an ambush every minute!'

'No,' he said to me. 'You can't go with us. Don't forget Black Jack! You aren't even supposed to be in camp!'

But in the face of my insistence—and perhaps also because it amused him to put my physical resistance to the test, he relented:

'If the *day-uy* is willing to take you with his group, I can't say anything. Don't forget that we are officially only "advisers",' he pointed out with the hint of a smile.

'All right,' said the *day-uy*, 'I'll take her.'

And at Tony's suggestion, carried unanimously, the operation was called 'Michèle'.

'But you come on one condition,' Maple added. 'Learn how to handle an M-16 and a grenade.'

'No. It's out of the question for me to be armed. I'm not making war but a film—I'm an *observer*.'

'I'm not asking you to carry a weapon, but to learn how to use one. I'm sorry, it's a compulsory condition. This is not a major American operation backed up by planes, artillery, and hundreds, maybe thousands of men. This is a commando operation.'

My short-sight, plus my natural repulsion to firearms, made me a wretched pupil.

The last briefing before departure was held exclusively for the Americans. Vietnamese officers were deliberately excluded.

Wednesday evening, 1800 hours

Maple and his team are ready to embark. With uniforms camouflaged and brush on their helmets, they look just like Boy Scouts. Each has four days' rations, a hammock, a blanket, grenades, flares, smoke bombs, an M.16 and daggers.

They must land on the beach at the north of the island before sunrise: about five o'clock in the morning.

Group Number Two—*my* group—must get going at midnight.

But first to set the characters and the scene:

The day-uy: speaks no English, but colloquial French; was an adjutant in the French Army; about thirty-five years old, rather heavy, stocky. He pretends to agree with everything the Americans decide to do, but he is only paying them lip-service. A hypocrite? Yes. But perhaps he also understands the limitations of his men.

His lieutenant: small, slim and younger, twenty-six years old. Impulsive by nature, he has a lot of influence with his captain. Fanatically anti-American with a really bitter jealousy. Always with the *day-uy* in camp. Never seen them eating in the American mess.

Lieutenant Levin: twenty-six years old, tall, blond. A perfect product of American education. Newly-married, and fresh out of West Point. With nothing like the experience of a Maple, he tries hard to 'catch on'. Makes superhuman efforts to communicate with the Vietnamese and to speak their language. Has respect and a great admiration for his captain.

'He's the only guy I know that I'd be scared of if he said to me one day "I'm going to kill you",' he confided to me.

His chief asset: an enthusiasm that can sometimes make up for inexperience.

Sergeant Doug Grantham: the radio operator. Follows Levin and approves any decision he makes.

Now for the setting: hills and mountains covered by dense jungle. Thousands of leeches and steel traps. In the valley, which runs almost the whole length of the island, many pepper plantations, one of its chief resources.

The Action: For Group No. 2 departure as arranged at midnight, behind the landing-strip.

No moon, but a sky full of stars. I haven't got time to dream. Walking in single file, I am far too busy keeping up with the man in front, trying to step in his footprints. One thought obsesses me: the memory of the paperweight in the office back at camp, a cement base with metal points about six inches long, in the shape of a fish hook. They say that the territory we're crossing is full of them!

We join hands so that we won't lose one another as we plunge deeper into the forest. No more stars now, only the black night . . . and the contact of two hands. Like Tom Thumb, those in front leave a trail of phosphorescent twigs on the path to guide us. Progress is slow and difficult. Our hands and arms are covered in scratches, our jackets already torn that first night, and the next day continues in the same way.

Every time we halt, Levin sprays himself with repellent but repellent or not, we are all stung by mosquitoes or ants. The worst thing is the leeches. They cling to our skin and suck our blood greedily. Then we have to burn them with a cigarette. A knife would be the quickest solution, but it leaves a permanent scar.

And all the time, this terror of an ambush, which obsesses us all. A suspicious sound, and we fling ourselves flat on our stomachs, the men's fingers on the triggers, mine on the camera release. False alarms!

Once, however, . . .

'It's nothing. Only a cobra.'

A cobra more than twelve feet long! 'Only a cobra', indeed! If we were not at war that cobra by itself would make an adventure story.

After killing it, the soldiers dragged it along with them hoping, I think, to feast on it in camp. But a few hours later the stench even two yards away was unbearable. Luckily a skirmish on the last day forced them, at last, to leave it behind.

Towards evening, tension began to grow between the *day-uy* and Levin. Although we had been walking all day, we had also made innumerable detours, often advancing crabwise.

The rendezvous fixed by Maple was still far off, and the way we were going we would never reach it at the appointed time.

At six o'clock, the *day-uy* decided to halt, against the advice of Levin who wanted to go on for three or four hours more. He kept on arguing even after the trenches had been dug and camp pitched for the night. We all slept in hammocks slung between the trees. But with the torrential rains, they quickly turned into bathtubs, in spite of our ponchos which gave us absurdly small protection. We set off again at six o'clock in the morning, frozen to the bone.

Detours, halts, more detours, more halts! Impossible to make radio contact with 'Thunderball' (Maple's code name). Levin's anxiety increased, and map in hand, he kept saying, 'We'll never make the rendezvous. They're counting on us. If they meet serious trouble, they'll never get out of it. We'll be too far away to do anything. We must make it!'

But conversation was more than usually difficult between Levin, who made desperate efforts to make himself understood in Vietnamese, and the *day-uy*, who made no effort at all and even looked amused.

An ideal interpreter, speaking French and English, I was taken aside, by both, each wanting me to act as judge—a role I refused to accept.

Levin: 'He's afraid. He doesn't want to go too far into a territory where he's never been in action.'

While Levin was speaking, the *day-uy* turned casually to me and, looking me straight in the eye, said with perfect calm, 'I hate Americans. They always want to make decisions.'

'You are entitled to your opinion,' I said, 'but there's one thing I don't understand. You agreed during the briefing, to make your way to the rendezvous, as arranged. The others are waiting for you. Maple is counting on you. Why didn't you give your reasons then for refusing to go now.'

'As you, too, were at the briefing,' the *day-uy* replied, 'you must have noticed that they didn't ask me what I thought of the plan or the way it should be carried out.'

Tension which goes on mounting poisons the atmosphere—and Levin, driven too far, suddenly announced:

'OK! I'll go to the rendezvous alone with the radio operator and only four or five men.'

'Just as you like.' And the *day-uy* calmly finished eating his bowl of rice and lay down for his siesta, though we were due to leave again in half an hour. As for Levin, he simply couldn't rest. Pacing around in a circle, he tried to contact Thunderball by radio, without success. He had spoken in a moment of understandable exasperation, but he knew he could not go on alone. It would be madness.

'All right, *day-uy*! I'm sorry. I know I'm only an "adviser"! You make the decisions.'

In spite of this apparent reconciliation—on one side an attempt to understand, on the other a small victory—the real problem was still unsolved: we were not going—or at least not going fast enough, and still making interminable detours—to the place of the rendez-vous.

The F.A.C.* observation plane that relays radio messages dropped us some batteries, as ours were definitely flat. They fell into the only swamp in the area, and it took us two hours to recover them.

All through the day, the heat was unbearable, but at night it always rained. Frozen, and soaked to the skin, the men all looked a little seedier each morning—unshaven, and eaten by mosquitoes and leeches. My own state was just as bad—I was completely exhausted.

From the top of Headquarters Hill, Doug finally made contact with Thunderball, who was furious. Because of our delay, a new rendezvous was fixed, on the far side of the valley near a little village.

Forest, stream, valley, forest, hill, valley. . . . At last, about six in the evening we reached the meeting point: three houses—obviously abandoned only a short time ago—between two hills.

Team No. 1 was not due to arrive until the next morning.

Against Levin's advice, the *day-uy* prepared his own ambush: a platoon would spend the night, posted on each hill. His lieutenant,

* F.A.C.: Forward Aircraft Control.

Vietnam: rice field after rice field; a people who laugh in spite of everything;
street markets.

Difficulties and obstacles, but more important, tremendous good nature, as long as you're far away from the American camps. Near them, you must pay for everything, even a helping hand: every kilometre is expensive.

Bad roads and ferry boats: you don't get ahead very quickly but at least you have time to talk and make friends.

One bridge, two bridges, three bridges—all destroyed.

A Regular Army patrol on the Dalat road, one kilometre before the Vietcong toll post. The one acting the fool and laughing is showing off a chicken he's just stolen in the neighbourhood.

Somewhere in the Delta, I come across a Buddhist funeral. Immediately they invite me to it, and put on a pantomime in my honour.

Every morning Sophie makes a tour of the airfield in a little American plane. Her parents own a plantation at Blao, on the edge of the Vietcong zone. Her brother, who is ten, wants to go to France 'because there's no war'.

The roads belong to the Americans. There's an unending stream of arms and materials.

The Orient Express! I come across convoys of five hundred trucks.

'Don't say you're a journalist. We'd rather believe you're a tourist.' An advance artillery post near the Cambodian frontier.

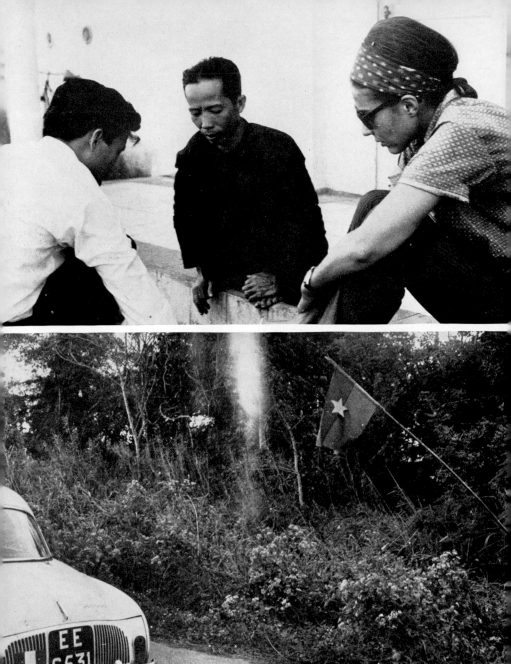

A Vietcong defects: naturally, he's never touched a gun nor a grenade.

The Vietcongs were at the Christmas rendezvous. Between Ninh Hao and Ban Me Thuot, I was inspected by a Vietcong post. A kilometre further on, this N.L.F. flag.

with the help of two soldiers, was killing chickens. Hot soup tonight!

One problem: if Thunderball and his team were ahead of time, they ran the risk of falling into the *day-uy*'s trap. As it was impossible to contact them, Levin and Doug also set off to the ambush to prevent any mistake. No one was caught in the trap, but the rain once more kept its rendezvous with us that night.

Towards ten o'clock next morning the *day-uy* grew impatient:

'If we can't make radio contact with Thunderball before two o'clock this afternoon, we're going back to camp.'

Levin and Doug were biting their nails. At two o'clock exactly, as in a corny novel, contact was finally made.

'We're on "Charlie's" heels. Go two kilometres from your present position and cut them off,' ordered Maple.

It was not, after all, under cover of the jungle, but on a pepper plantation, that the skirmish took place, backed by the F.A.C. and its rockets. Two hours later, the valley was quiet again, and the two groups reunited.

We joined up with Thunderball and his men. Americans, Vietnamese—all were naked from the waist up and completely covered with leech bites. A man called Sam had lost his pants—they'd been torn to pieces. Exhausted by their march through the jungle, they were also over-excited by the battle they'd just been fighting.

On reaching the plain the Vietnamese soldiers hurled themselves, shouting, on some cows, which they promptly slaughtered, cutting their throats and slitting open their stomachs. They slashed and cut. A blazing sun, and the smell of blood. Gleefully, they plunged their hands into the gaping carcasses. Pieces of meat and intestines, dripping with blood, hung from their knapsacks. I was nauseated, but I forced myself to take pictures.

A suspicious sound. The six mercenaries disappeared at the double.

Ten minutes later Doug came to look for me.

'Bring your camera. Maple wants you.'

They were all standing round the two abandoned houses.

'They were firing at the observation plane from in there. They almost hit it, the bastards!'

'Matches! A lighter! Take pictures! Look at the American mercenaries who burn down houses! Go on! Burn everything! You'll get some lovely shots!'

Dн

Nerves on edge, Maple scarcely knew what he was saying. I felt as if I were taking part in some great epic film, some wide-screen western. And I wanted only one thing, to shout, 'Cut!'

We are started back to camp together. No detours, this time, but the shortest route, via the valley and the landing strip. There was not much risk of an ambush now.

One kilometre farther on, two houses, three children: two boys and a girl.

'Tony! Where's my interpreter? Come here!' yelled Maple. 'Ask them where their parents are . . . Ah, V.C., of course! O.K. Bring the children along. Burn the houses. I don't want anything left!'

I collected the three children, and persuaded them to come with us. The little girl, about six years old, roused my admiration. Very proud and erect, she trotted along as fast as she could on her bare feet. Like a little woman, she looked after her two smaller brothers, at the same time. Head held high, she tried hard not to cry. But though she managed to hold back her tears, she could not help turning her little head from time to time to look back at her blazing home.

Five hundred yards, half a mile, one mile . . . one, two, four, ten, twenty more houses. Women, children, a few old men . . . and always the same orders. I began to realize that Maple was not joking and that he really intended to destroy everything in his path.

'Five minutes for them to collect what they want and then fire the houses!'

Carrying one child in my arms, I placed myself at the head of the column, and as we went along I sent each new group of women and children to join the other refugees.

I don't know what they must have thought at seeing a woman in uniform, but Maple with his M.16 and his bellowings terrified them!

The children cried, and screamed. I'd packed up my camera long before, and now found myself with a child in each arm plus a third on my knapsack. Little girls of four or five carried their younger brothers or sisters. The women struggled with bundles they'd hastily thrown together. When night came, it was still more difficult, with the little ones stumbling on the stones. Sudden explosions made us all jump—ammunition or arms hidden in the houses, burnt, too!

Two hours later, Maple joined our group and, seeing how exhausted we were, made the column halt. He ordered us to rest.

The F.A.C. sent us some beer, and lemonade.

Maple was no longer the same man. Calmly, quietly, gently, he looked after the children, and comforted them. He talked to the women in Vietnamese. I gazed at him in astonishment! I scarcely recognized him!

It was well after midnight when we finally arrived at our point of departure—the landing strip.

The leader of the district, who was waiting for us, raised his arms to heaven and protested,

'What are we going to do with them? And the plantations! They're one of the principal sources of wealth on the island. If there are no more houses, there'll be no more people to look after the plantations!'

'We'll take all necessary measures,' Maple told him, anxious to put an end to the 'whys' and 'hows'. 'Meanwhile, the refugees are going to spend the night here. I'll have bedding and rice sent down from the camp.'

One hour later 'Thunderball', alias Maple, reported by radio to 'Black Jack', alias Kelly, the results of Operation Michèle, as follows:

'We didn't find a hospital or an ammunition dump, as we expected. But instead:

Twelve thousand kilos of rice—too far away to carry back, so we threw it in the river:

One political training school found and destroyed. The documents captured, including a plan of our camp correct to the smallest detail, and also our plan of attack.

In the course of today's engagement: fifteen V.C.s killed.

Rifles recovered—two.

On the way back: forty houses destroyed and burnt.

We have collected sixty-three refugees: women and children and a few old men.

No losses on our side; one man slightly wounded.

Worth noting: the attitude of the *day-uy*, who did not make the rendezvous as arranged.

For the moment, the head of the district is looking after the refugees.

Tomorrow I'll be sending you a list of what we need—top priority.'

And, in answer to a question from Black Jack:

'Yes, we had to destroy the houses. If not, "Victor Charlie" could have gone on getting fresh supplies. Our whole operation today would have gone for nothing. I must point out that ammunition was hidden in those houses. Ammunition that exploded as they burnt.'

I was still not supposed to be in camp at all, much less to have been in action. So I left next day on a Caribou for Cantho. I was the only passenger apart from the outgoing captain.

He made no comment on the operation. He just said to me, very sadly:

'I'm sorry you couldn't have come a month earlier. Your report would have been different. But I was not considered energetic enough! So I've got to return to Fort Bragg for a tour of duty. I'm going back to Hell!'

Three months later I returned to Phu Ghoc. There were three Special Forces camps under the command of Maple, who had been promoted to major. The refugees were still there. More of them.

5

'We're Winning the War'

The Marines, not averse to publicity, know how to look after the press! At Da Nang, their principal base in Vietnam, all journalists are given a roneoed fifteen-page document which states that the Marines were:

The first American troops engaged in the war.

The first arm of the service to wipe out an important Vietcong unit in battle.

The first to use a field aerodrome.

The first to install Hawk rockets in a battle zone.

The first to organize a vast programme of civilian aid.

And finally, the first to undertake combined action with the local 'Home Guard'.

Their report ends with the categorical statement: 'We are winning the war.'

Since March 1966, since the time of the Buddhist revolt, of General Thi and the attack on the American base, General Lewis W. Walt, commanding the 3rd Marine Amphibian Force, has declared Da Nang out of bounds for his 57,000 soldiers, spread over the five provinces of the 1st Army Corps from Quang Ngai to the Demilitarized Zone.

But the M.P.s who patrol the streets and see the girls in the bars wistfully sipping their tea should take a look on the other side of the counter; that's where the G.I.s are, crouching on the floor. Every now and then a hand appears, fumbles for a glass, and snatches it quickly out of sight.

In the streets, you can't put a pin between the souvenir shops. And, just like in Saigon, on trestles, on the pavement, there is also a black market.

The day after my arrival, the city was hung with flags. A bicycle race in several stages—from Da Nang to the Demilitarized Zone, and on to the bridge of Ben Hoî—was announced. A four-day race with seventy starters! It is a mini 'Tour de France'. Organized by the Government to launch the electoral campaign; and pennants with 'Vote on September 11th' flew beside those announcing the race. I rented a Renault 2CV which would only go forward in jerks. With six of us piled into it we started out to wait for the riders at a point nine miles away near a bridge, which was both a road and railway bridge, and which was held and guarded day and night by the Marines.

Here they come! But instead of publicity caravans there are tanks. Then come armoured jeeps, and after that the cyclists. There are only sixteen of them left. The winner of the day before wears a yellow jersey, as is customary.

Surrounded by tanks that nearly run us down, we do our best to follow this crazy race. As the cyclists flash past, the children shout encouragement, and the women throw water in their faces!

They finish with a flourish: crowds, wreaths of flowers, kisses for the winner. Congratulations from General Lam, commander of the 1st Army Corps, and from General Walt, and finally the national anthem. No one has been kidnapped by the Vietcong, but just before Huê, in the direction of the 'street without joy', as the French called it, there's been fighting. To leave the road free for the race, twelve dead Vietcong were kicked into a ditch.

That evening I dined with the French Consul. He talked to me about three coffee plantations at Khê Sanh* near the Laotian border and the Ho Chi Minh Trail. The planters are completely isolated, except for a Special Forces Camp. Dong Ha has been closed, and they no longer have any way of getting their produce out.

'I have just come from there with General Walt,' he said. 'He is very understanding. He promised to have the harvest transported by military aircraft.'

The consul went on: 'A French garage owner from Huê—and by the way, you must visit the temples of the Imperial City—who was on the road after nine o'clock at night ran into an ambush. He was wounded, and so was his driver. After cursing them for being on the road so late, the Viets let them go on, bleeding profusely, to the nearest Government post.'

* That is where eight months later the greatest battle of the Vietnam war to date took place, the battle of Hill 881, the Poilane plantation, called after its owner.

The next day I went to something rather special—the Marines call it a 'county fair'.

In a village cleared—or so they hope—of all traces of the enemy by the military operations of the last few days, two companies set to work at dawn. First they search the houses thoroughly, and all the bushes round about, in case of possible traps. After that, they bring in the provisions: rice, to each family, cakes of soap cut in half to prevent them from appearing, two days later, on the black market; school books. The sanitary squads take care of the sick, nurse them, and try to teach them the A.B.C. of hygiene.

For the children this is the event of the week. They stand in line, their legs oozing with pus; a medical orderly swabs them with a brush which he dips into a bucket of disinfectant.

Then, under the blazing sun, the children queue up by the reservoir. Each one is given a toothbrush, a piece of soap, and a paper drinking cup. The dentist arrives. In his left hand he holds a denture; in his right hand, a toothbrush. He brushes the denture vigorously, giving a running commentary as he does so, the children gurgle with delight. The interpreter shouts for order and, to encourage them, brushes his own teeth, also!

Blue skies, scorching heat and music while you work! Yes, indeed! The band is there, too! Even the littlest ones clap their hands round the big drum.

Apart from spreading the image of the 'American way of life', the Marines have realized that there's little point in winning the war if the people are not behind them. So these professional soldiers, these mercenaries, have been turned into peacemakers. The Combined Action Companies were born.

The People's Forces—or village militia—are without doubt the worst troops in South Vietnam. They have the reputation of shooting birds and fleeing at the first sound of enemy fire. But the Marines— all volunteers after six months in Vietnam—now stay in the villages. They live, eat, and fight with the People's Forces. They train them and try to gain the confidence of the people they protect—and they help them to build schools, bridges, and markets. In short, they have created a sort of Military Peace Corps.

At Dong Ha, the Marine base nearest the Demilitarized Zone, which runs alone the 17th Parallel and cuts Vietnam in half, I found the Schoendoerffers. Pierre was there to make a film for television. He wanted to tell the story of American unity, and had chosen a group of 'flying cavaliers', belonging to the 1st Division of Airborne Cavalry. His wife, Pat, was with him. I had known them in Paris. Pierre had finished his film and had come on here to see how the American Marines fight.

With their hair very short—for they had shaved their heads on their arrival in Vietnam—and their uniforms soiled by two months' campaigning, Pierre, Dominique Merlin, his cameraman, and the sound engineer, Raymond Adam, look like any nondescript G.I.s. As for Pat, also in khaki, she was sporting a sky-blue rain hat that had the most astonishing effect in the midst of all this green jungle and grey mud.

We were more than twenty in the hut that served as a press camp. It smelled of wild animals and damp wool in spite of the 'Miss Dior' —found in the camp P.X.—which I sprayed conscientiously twice a day. We were waiting for something big to break. But for four days, it had been impossible for the planes to take off because of the heavy rain. The monsoon kept the American air forces grounded. There was nothing we could do about it, so we played poker—with bullets for chips.

'There are enough of us here to make up a platoon,' cracked Sean Flynn in exasperation. He is Errol Flynn's son. For months he hung around Marine camps studying their habits for a part he had been promised. The producer finally gave it to another actor, and Sean went to Singapore to make a film. Now he has come back to the Marines quite voluntarily, to please himself, because he really likes war.

Every evening, General English, with his kind smile, would tell us:

'Sorry, boys. Operation postponed.' And all because of this blessed rain that never stops flooding the Annamese Ranges.

The sick-bay was right behind our hut. One evening, towards midnight, we were petrified, our breath caught in our throats, and our stomachs tight with fear at the terrifying screams of a G.I. who had just been brought in after stepping on a mine. As he left the Air Force Club, he had tried to take a short cut across the fields to the road again and had foolishly walked into the trap.

In spite of zero visibility, a helicopter took off to carry him to the hospital ship, which was cruising near the coast. The pilot came

back in tears. The wounded man was his best friend, and they were
going to have to amputate both legs and an arm.

Pat and I decided to leave Pierre and his crew and return to
Da Nang where, so rumour had it, President Johnson was due to
arrive shortly.

At the new press camp, we were greeted with cheers.

'Two French girls! Our unit's in luck!'

It was oppressively hot. Captain Stackpool sent for a jeep to drive
us to the beach that borders the China Sea; an immense beach of
fine sand. On a hundred yards of it, enclosed by barbed wire, and
guarded by M.P.s, the troops can bathe. To say that our arrival
passed unnoticed would not be true. Fifteen hands reached out to
offer us iced beer.

'Take mine, it's colder. . . . I'm Mike . . . Jack, John or Frank. . . .'

They were airmen, sailors, or Marines.

'Come and share our barbecue! We've got some enormous steak.
We must be dreaming! Two French girls! Aren't you afraid of the
war?'

'No. Not on the beach!'

We could hear the thunder of jets breaking the sound barrier
and, in the distance, the guns. When we left, fifty men crowded
round to say 'au revoir' and wave to us.

Accompanied by two American journalists—Joe Hardy, not yet
married, and Esther Clark—this was by no means her first war!
—I visited a captured Vietcong village which had been recon-
structed with all its booby-traps and was now used for training
recruits.

The instructors saw us coming! Usually they're content with
showing journalists over the village and pointing out the various
traps which might claim the G.I. if he walks through the jungle
without looking where he's going. For us, they put on a big show.
There were traps like nobody's business!

'Come in!' said the sergeant, gallantly inviting us to go ahead of
him. Bang! The gate exploded. One small village, and about fifty
traps! We put our right foot carefully on the ground, but the left
foot did not 'see' the wire hidden in the grass. Bang! We avoided
one trap only to walk into or jump back from another. Bang! Bang!
To get our breath back, we sat down on a bench in the house. It
blew up! Thoroughly shaken, we escaped from this military 'Luna

Park'. And for the next forty-eight hours all three of us made a detour every time we saw an empty jam tin on the ground.

Pierre and his men joined us at Da Nang, and we all took off for An Khê.

'Why don't you land at Pleiku?' shouted Pierre, trying to make himself heard above the thundering of the C-130's engines. 'Perhaps you could find a convoy and join us again by road. It's very beautiful.'

At Pleiku the first thing we did was to try to find Leslie Smith. Born in Vietnam of English missionary parents, he was once a professional hunter. Now he has become a naturalized American. He works for the J.U.S.P.A.O. and is concerned with psychological warfare in this region of high plateaux which he knows like the back of his hand, speaking three or four mountain dialects.

There had just been a bad moment. When the Secretary of Defense, McNamara, asked him, with an over-confident smile:

'Are we on the way to winning the war?'

Leslie had replied, 'No! Not here in the highlands!'

Unfortunately, Leslie was not in Pleiku.

'He must be somewhere in the jungle with his mountain boys', Lieutenant Duchesne, the press officer, told us. 'But if you want to go by road to An Khê, there's a convoy every afternoon at three. It's a petrol convoy. Come along, I'll take you to the starting place.'

The convoy was about to set off. We climbed aboard under the amused gaze of the G.I.s and a few mountain children.

We perched ourselves on an enormous tanker. Our twenty-year-old driver wore a bulletproof vest and a helmet. The countryside might have been beautiful, but it was submerged in the black smoke that poured from the truck ahead of us and from a few hundred others ahead of it.

'Is the road quiet?'

'Yes. I've been on this route for six months. It's marvellous. Nothing ever happens, and it's so beautiful.' Then he went on, 'There are plaques all the way along commemorating the destruction of one of your units, but we can't stop now, and in any case, they're hidden in the undergrowth.'

Yes. It was the G.M. 100 (Groupe Mobile 100). Mainly veterans from the Korean Battalion. In June 1954, while they were defending the fortified town of An Khê they found themselves faced with the alternative of holding on and provoking another Dien Bien Phu or falling back on Pleiku at the risk of having another Cao Bang. It was on June 25, I think, just about here, that the Vietminh ambushed them. It was a slow and awful death. . . .

'From a helicopter you can still see the remains of trucks and tanks. . . .'

He braked violently. In all the noise and smoke we had not realized what was happening. The front of the convoy had been attacked. There were several dead and wounded. Armoured jeeps rushed up and down the column. Drivers, crouched behind the wheels of their trucks, kept a watch on the jungle.

Pat had said to me, 'Pierre is involved with the war, not me. I hang about in the background and as the war is everywhere, I'm in it too. Sometimes more than he is. He's always looking for the action but he doesn't always find it. As for me, I don't look for it, and I always end up behind the front line where things happen.'

And that's just where we were—behind the front line!

Light helicopters machine-gunned the roadside, and two large ones landed near us. The men leaped out, rifles at the ready. I made a film of it.

'You'd do better if you took the cover off the lens,' Pat chuckled. The light was almost gone.

'We may have to spend the night here,' our driver announced. 'We can fill ourselves up with biscuits and peanut butter—which is better, or at least not as bad, as C-rations.' It was completely dark by the time the convoy set off again.

The leader of the convoy made us ride in an ambulance—he said, 'You'll be more protected from bullets here.'

At An Khê we met the boys again and told them our saga. They were furious and green with envy at having missed it all.

An Khê is the base camp of the First Cavalry Division (Air-mobile). It is the most modern unit in the whole army, and also the most mobile, with 500 helicopters. It is a complete division, that is, 18,000 men. The camp is the cleanest, the most hygienic, the most obviously 'made in the U.S.A.' in all Vietnam. There are often small wooden houses instead of tents, there are several little chapels, also of wood, and an open-air theatre arranged in tiers, where Jayne Mansfield and other pin-ups have appeared. There are a few little villas as well surrounded by lawns that find it difficult to grow.

A laundryman in the village had been recommended to us, M. Brutus. His shop was called 'Pretty Lilly'. It wasn't easy to find; there are more than 200 laundries in An Khê, lined up all along the road between the base and the village. Every second house is a laundry, called 'Number One', 'Lovely', and so on.

After three months in Vietnam, the 'flying cavaliers' realized that the only way to avoid Vietcong spies was to deny all Vietnamese access to the camp. Result: the G.I. carries his own laundry to the village to be washed. We finally found M. Brutus hidden behind piles of dirty linen. His wife, bent over a sewing machine, was sewing on stripes and badges that had to be removed for the wash. The G.I.s dump their sacks and sit down all over the place. The washer-women offer them Coca Cola, the children cling to their legs or bounce on their knees. Each soldier has his favourite shop which he is used to, and where he's treated like a friend of the family.

Sitting in armchairs underneath pictures of Brigitte Bardot and Jane Fonda, we watch all the coming and going.

A sun-tanned American soldier arrives and asks for his bundle in French. His name is 'La Violette', and he's from Louisiana. Where he comes from, everyone speaks French.

Another G.I. comes in. He, too, asks for his laundry in French. This one is Canadian.

And now a Negro who also asks for his laundry—always in French. Pat and I look at each other in bewilderment.

'Come on,' Pat says to me, 'Let's go and find Pierre and the boys.'

Fifty wooden huts arranged in a horseshoe with gaudy notices. In the centre a souvenir stand selling sandwiches, dolls, and key rings. It's all enclosed with barbed wire. An M.P. in a sentry box guards the entrance, demanding everyone's credentials: identity card and contraceptive.

We modestly settled for our press cards! When he saw us coming, the M.P. turned his head, opened his eyes wide, then looked the other way, blushing with embarrassment, and muttering,

'This isn't the sort of place I'd like my wife to be walking around.'

We would never have believed it! It wasn't the G.I.s we had to be afraid of . . . but those ladies! They were wildly excited and are probably still talking about our visit. Backed up against a hut we were overwhelmed with caresses. They wanted to touch us, to kiss us. As for the boys, they were doubled up with laughter and taking shots of us! When the women had calmed down a little, they made us go into one of the bistros. They wanted to know all about us. They offered us beer, Coca Cola . . . anything we liked. Three thousand sailors on an aircraft carrier were not half so enterprising!

That evening we went on patrol in helicopters armed with rockets. Bulletproof vests and helmets were compulsory.

'Are you all right, Pat and Michèle?' asked the pilot. 'Your helmets are connected by radio. Press the button when you want to talk.'

Every time a rocket was shot off, the din was infernal and made us jump. I took pictures.

'What's really exciting,' a pilot said to me on another mission, 'is to fly solo or by twos over a village suspected of being Vietcong. If we are fired on, we call up our buddies! Then the V.C. get a rain of fire on their heads! You ought to see "Charlie" run in the rice fields.'

'And tonight,' asked Pat, 'what are we looking for?'

'Nothing. Just a routine flight. We fire at random in the jungle.'

At the airfield next day we waited for the plane for Saigon. This time we were not the only women. There was also a young girl in a sky-blue dress, with a basket on her arm. She belonged to the Red Cross.

'There are six of us at An Khê.'

'What do you do?'

'We organize games for the soldiers. We also have a club where they can listen to records, write letters, talk to us. We work at the forward bases. We bring them sweets.'

It is 'Operation Charm'.

The girls are between twenty-one and twenty-six years old. Wearing dresses and make-up, they always look as if they've just come out of a bandbox. You'll find them at all the main bases. They don't belong to the Army, but come to Vietnam for a year, as volunteers. And, of course, almost all of them go back to the United States engaged.

Saigon was still hot, damp, humid, and dirty. With several French friends—the Americans don't dare venture out on the highroad— we went to Vungtao. In spite of the potholes and the convoys, in spite of the stretches where you have to drive flat out to dodge snipers' bullets, specially when crossing the plantations, many Saigonese still make the journey to Cap St. Jacques every weekend.

It is a rest-area for the troops. Every week a new hotel springs up and the kiosks along the beach are called 'Miami', 'Florida', or 'Las Vegas'.

Vungtao is an R and R (Rest and Relaxation) Zone—that's how the G.I.s refer to their leave. Many prefer Hong Kong, Singapore, Taipeh or Bangkok.

When I say 'beach', I really mean 'beaches'. First there's the beach for the Vietnamese—which is also the French beach. Coexistence works very well there. A little farther on is the Americans' beach, and beyond it is the R-and-R beach of the South Koreans.

Finally, the whole end of the immense bay belongs to the Australians.

With their enormous bush hats, the Australians look like Boy S outs . . . but very effective Boy Scouts! Calmly, without any publicity, they go about their business. They are the best soldiers for counter-guerrilla warfare: they learned their lessons in Malaysia.

Coming back along the road, we met other Boy Scouts, real ones this time—Vietnamese boys, about fifteen years old. They were returning from a picnic in the neighbourhood. A neighbourhood where war was raging!

We dared not be late getting back, for the road closes at six o'clock. After that the Vietnamese, both civilian and military, take refuge in the camps, surround themselves with thousands of yards of barbed wire, barricade themselves in, and sleep with one eye open until the next morning. These posts are often attacked.

In the bay, offshore, cruise forty, forty-five, forty-six merchant ships! Sometimes they have to wait for a month or even more before they can unload at Saigon. Held up within sight of Cap St. Jacques, the officers and men are prisoners on board.

The next day was a national holiday. For a whole week the troops had been drilling for this night. Ky was anxious for his parade to be a success.

With Pierre and his group, we were in our places by seven-thirty. The festival was due to begin at eight o'clock.

The first salvos were fired!

'Well! For once they've started early!'

More salvos, a pause, five minutes' hesitation. . . .

'Good heavens! It's mortar-fire! The "Viets" are attacking Saigon!' I ran towards the Grall Hospital. Shells had fallen in the courtyard, on the buildings.

Then, all was quiet. Ky arrived, looking very relaxed. Next came the cadets from the military school at Dalat, and while the 'Popular Youth' were marching past, shells rained down again. The 'Youth' broke ranks, ran for shelter . . . more bursts of mortar fire, then silence.

In the official stand, Thieu and Ky, in spite of their smiles, were tense. The last shell fell too close for comfort. Only fifty yards away!

The next day, the international press announced, 'The Vietcong bombarded the heart of Saigon!'

'Charlie' gained another point on the psychological front, the most important in this war of nerves.

PART II

On the Roads of Vietnam

EH

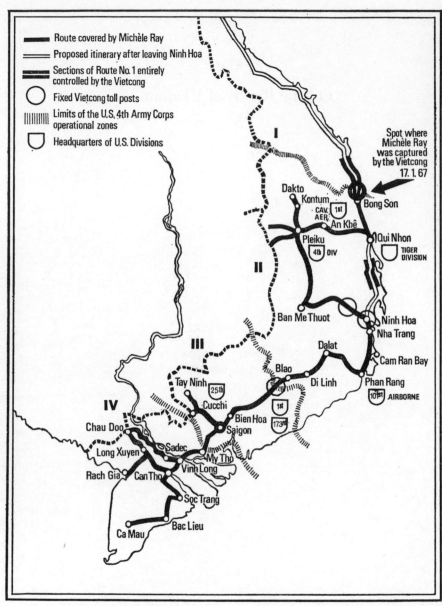

General map of Vietnam showing American and Vietcong positions
and the route taken by the author.

6

The Crazy Journey

It all began with the loan of a car in Saigon. I never imagined then that one day I would be travelling through South Vietnam by road. A first timid attempt—Saigon to Can Tho, about 110 miles—made me a heroine to the Americans. But to the people at Can Tho, it was just a routine trip, a journey they made every week.

In the words of one American correspondent: 'You have seen some interesting things by moving about in the Delta. Keep it up. See a lot. Go from Ca Mau to the 17th Parallel.' A challenge!

In spite of the confidence my first trips in the Delta had given me, the roads in Vietnam didn't seem practical unless I was willing to take what seemed to me enormous risks. However, after five months, by accompanying the Marines, the First Cavalry, the First and the Fourth Infantry Divisions, the Koreans, and finally the Vietnamese; and by taking planes and helicopters, following convoys, and going on route marches, my attitude changed.

I sought information from Americans, Vietnamese, drivers and others, and from French planters. I also interrogated Vietcong prisoners. From all these various sources, my own views began to take shape, and assert themselves. I knew the roads the convoys took, and those controlled by the 'Viets', at what points they collected toll and where there was danger of mines. And one day, after the 'five o'clock follies', on the terrace of the Continental Hotel, between two iced teas, I announced in a very firm tome:

'I'm going to drive from Ca Mau to the Demilitarized Zone by car. I'm not out to set a record, or to prove anything. I just want to see for myself, to get to know the country. I've followed almost all the units, in the area. I don't think I can learn any more by going on with it. I have enough pictures of troops. What I want now is to see the people, the Vietnamese.'

The journalists' reaction:

'In two weeks or a month we'll still be here. Drinking the same tea, the same beer. And we'll say then, "Remember that French girl . . . Michèle? She was a nice girl. Too bad she had to get blown up by a mine! We knew it would happen. . . . By the way, who was that new girl at the briefing this afternoon?" '

And so life would go on.

They joked, they tried to frighten me, they treated me like a harmless nut-case. I tried to explain. 'I've taken all the advice I can. I can do it—it's a risk, but a calculated risk.' I talked, I gave examples. I began to get annoyed—or I was met with either a brick-wall attitude, or indulgent smiles. Two or three of them, though, admitted I was right: among others, Zalin B. Grant, correspondent for *Time* magazine. For the last two years he had been the only journalist in Vietnam who spoke Vietnamese, and he was to become my technical adviser.

'It'll make a good story,' he said, 'and if anyone has a chance of succeeding, she has; she's French, a journalist, and a woman—a trump card. She's the exact opposite of a combatant.'

I was ready to leave when I ran into an unexpected problem. The manager of the Renault* company objected.

'The risks are great,' he insisted, 'and precisely because you're Renault's "blue-eyed girl" we must notify Paris and get their consent.'

In Paris they'd say no. I was sure of it. All the car-hire agents made it clear: 'Only for Saigon. Insurance companies won't cover accidents of war like the vehicle being blown up by a mine, or stolen by the Vietcong!'

Someone suggested: 'Buy a scooter. The risks are less—only two wheels instead of four!'

One Frenchman, the owner of a garage, who'd been in Saigon for twenty years, was enthusiastic about my project.

'I'll lend you a "mini-moke",' he offered. 'You're right. Vietnam is a marvellous country and the only way to get to know it well is to travel by road.'

A 'mini-moke'? Yes, fine. But it looks too like a jeep, too military. As a matter of elementary security I had to have an ordinary civilian car. I couldn't afford to buy one and, in any case they were very hard to get, as imports were restricted. The prices were

* In 1965, I had organized a rally, 'Tierra del Fuego to Alaska', with two 4L Renaults.

exorbitant: 650,000 piastres for a Dauphine, the equivalent of £2,500!

I jotted down an estimate of what I would need and sent it to Renault in Paris. As I wanted to persuade them, I tried to make it funny.

'The risks: being blown up by a mine, running into an ambush, getting captured, getting killed . . . I'll skip the rest!

'Don't say "she's crazy," please read on.

'Two kinds of mines:

'Contact mines: I'll try to leave those for the next man by not driving before nine o'clock in the morning. I'll never drive at night, as all the roads belong to "Victor Charlie" then.

'As for remote-controlled mines: they are, as a general rule, intended for military vehicles. Sometimes if the Vietcong want to impress the "local civilian" population for one reason or another, they blow up some public transport vehicle . . . with twenty passengers or more!

'But a Dauphine with only one person aboard? I don't want to annoy you or to underestimate myself, but a Claymore mine deserves a bigger prize than that!

'Running into an ambush: the wisest solution is to keep clear of military convoys, which are their main objectives! To avoid meeting them is obviously more difficult.

'Making unfortunate contacts: at present there are in all Vietnam only two checkpoints either fixed, or variable—a kind of toll. The Vietcong, like tax collectors, are there every day, to pocket the duty on goods or passengers. Private cars are apparently exempt.

'The first V.C. checkpoint is between Saigon and Dalat—eighty to a hundred miles from here. The few French professors of the Dalat school who use the road from time to time have so far not had any difficulties. The second checkpoint: between Ninh Hoa and Ban Me Huot.

'Vietnamese civilians get by. But foreigners—only two European missionaries have passed that way in the last six months. To give myself every chance, I therefore plan to drive over the road during a truce: either at Christmas or the New Year.

'Undoubtedly the most dangerous area lies between Bong Son and Quang Ngai: territory completely in the hands of the National Liberation Front. The road is closed. There, for the first time, I'll have to load the car on a boat or a plane. But if there is the slightest chance of crossing this section by road, *I shall do it.*

'Danger of being captured: I hold to the principle that the Vietcong are orderly and disciplined. Once captured and handed over to the organization, assuming I am not drilled full of holes by an over-zealous soldier, I think that they will show me all the respect due to a woman and a journalist.

'However, an ambush, at any time or any place, a solitary sniper, the bands of pirates who pretend to be Vietcong, and rob and kill, an awkward mine, or some unforeseen accident . . . can result in your losing a car . . . and a dear friend!'

Eight days later I was given the green light.

'I am in receipt of your threatening letter and, as usual, we can only give in to you. We trust that your little rag will come up to expectations.'

The manager of the garage attended to my chief problem: mines. Four sand-bags in front, bulletproof vests inside the doors and under my seat, a five-millimetre steel plate behind both seats . . . they were ready to make the entire car bombproof!

At last I set off, on my 'crazy journey'. At each stop I wrote a long letter to Pat, who had gone back to Paris.

7

A Bench across the Road

My dear Pat,
Well, this is it! My 'crazy trip' has begun. I'm in Ca Mau, which really looks like the end of the world. If the French call the Delta 'The West', then this place with its one-storey wooden huts and its earth streets should be called 'The *Far* West'.

'Don't forget that, no matter what happens, your trip's going to be a real headache for me,' Lambroschini told me as we were having a last dinner in Saigon. 'At best, you'll get there. *They'll* note that you're French, all right, and therefore by assumption a friend of the Vietcong—for that reason only you'll be allowed through. Our position here, which is always dicey, is likely to get more unsettled still. If you're blown up by a mine, the recovery of your body won't be pleasant. And if you're captured, I'll have to try and make them release you. I'm speaking as the Consul General,' he added to clarify his own position. 'As plain Monsieur Lambroschini—"Good journey and good luck!" '

The A.F.P., among others, were all there to have a 'last' breakfast with me. They were not far from tears. George Page, the N.B.C correspondent, had come, too. But with a cameraman.

'You never know,' he said.

An encouraging farewell!

At the last moment, Raymond of the A.F.P. remarked: 'If I was going with you, I wouldn't be so worried!'

I didn't press him too hard, not wanting to be responsible for anyone else. No, I must be honest! In fact, whatever might happen, I thought I had a better chance of getting through if I were alone!

Saigon to Cantho! With the beginning of the dry season, the paddy fields were less flooded than in September. The women attended to the rice, their trousers rolled up to their thighs. As in Saigon itself, it was also the women who broke stones, cleared away the rubbish and repaired the roads. Madame Nhu was probably right to form her famous female militia. Tireless and strong, these Vietnamese women volunteers, with the fragile appearance of reeds, are just as tough.

I acted as a taxi for a bunch of A.B.C. boys.* They were filming a company of G.I.s as they emerged from a rice field with mud up to their waists. They had the drained, exhausted air of soldiers who are frustrated, searching for an enemy they never find, who slips through their fingers. They were part of the 25th Division, who had just dug themselves in at the boundary of the Fourth Tactical Zone, in other words the Delta, to clear the way for an expected mass landing of American troops.

In fact, do you know that General Quang, commander-in-chief of this zone—a man I admire immensely—has just been fired? By Ky, egged on by the Americans. But it's also due to the endless antagonism between the two clans: north and south.

The official charge is embezzlement. Actually, he was opposed to a massive concentration of American troops in the Delta. He wanted the war to remain Vietnamese, but with increased aid in planes and helicopters—there have obviously been too few of them up till now.

But his wife loved money—a clever woman, unequalled in business. She owned, among other things, the bars of the G.I.s—no, sorry, of the 'advisers'—at Cantho.

If embezzlement starts at the top, it's not really much use just sacking the head man. It goes right down the ladder, and all the rungs are rotten. A few officials are certainly honest, but they're lost in the crowd. They have neither the strength nor the will to make themselves heard, so they withdraw into themselves, and brood on their lost illusions.

On every bridge, and there are many of them, a few Vietnamese soldiers stand guard, looking as usual very relaxed about it. They dream, play cards or strum guitars, their legs hanging over the balustrade. As an afterthought, they cast an occasional eye over the nets which are there to deter floating mines.

These nets are a ludicrous protection. Almost all the bridges are duplicates—the first has been completely blown up. As for the temporary bridge, it's protected and guarded by a watch tower at both ends. Some few bridges, that have escaped the hands of Diem's

* American Broadcasting Corporation—an American television company.

wreckers, date from the French occupation. Thousands of yards of barbed wire surround them, and sand-bags. And here the two occupation eras meet: the old cement and blockhouse era, and the American era of barbed wire and sand-bags. In the Delta, perhaps more than anywhere else, the destruction of bridges proceeds at a much faster pace.

One bridge, two bridges, sometimes even a third bridge which replaces the replacement! Built of barges held together by metal plates, they can now, through constant practice, be installed very quickly. The technique of putting them together has been perfected.

A key road like route No. 4 is never closed for more than ten to twelve hours. Often five or six hours are enough to get the traffic moving again. This speed, though, doesn't prevent bottlenecks, which are inevitable in any case, since cars can only move in one direction at a time.

Beyond My Tho, the third emergency bridge was being built the evening I arrived. Taking advantage of the line of blocked cars, local enterprise had already had time to get organized. Women and children with trays on their heads, barefooted in the mud, but giggling madly all the same, picking their noses or chewing betel nut, offered us bananas, oranges, peeled grapefruit, or sliced pineapples strung on the end of a pole.

There was a school about fifty yards away. In the midst of all this commotion, a background noise of artillery and bursts of machine-gun fire, we could hear the children singing.

I can't think of Vietnam without immediately seeing children—hundreds and thousands of children. They spread out in what seems to me almost an unbroken line along the roads, their satchels in their hands or on their heads. They are an integral part of the landscape, much more so here in the Delta, where, because of the density of the population, they are in fact even more numerous. They are everywhere, they cling to you. The little girls sport very eccentric hats: large blue butterflies with wide-spread wings, or else an enormous rose, perched on the side of a sun-bonnet—'Junior Miss' fashion in the Vietnamese style.

At every ferry a hundred trucks, buses, or Lambrettas wait in a queue. In Paris when I was already concerned with Vietnam, headlines like 'Lambretta blown up by mine, 12 dead' always astonished me. By fitting them out with side-cars, the Vietnamese manage to pile more than a dozen on to them, not counting all the chickens and personal bundles.

The other means of transport is the motor-coach—dilapidated buses patched together with bits of string or wire. Always over-loaded, with goods piled on the roof, they tear along. The only thing to do is get out of the way. The driver has a mate at the back of the bus who leans right out of the window, half stupefied by the air rushing past, whistling, shouting, gesticulating, as though to say: 'Look out! Here we come; clear the countryside!' There are many accidents, and I don't mean only accidents of war!

Round the ferries, in the shanty-bistros, Coca Cola and American cigarettes of all kinds lie side by side with Chinese soup or *cah gio*. A boy snatched fifty piastres from me but he dashed back breathless, with my ferry ticket . . . and the change. I was furious at first, then I was touched.

Each ferry carries its blind man, its polio victim, its leper, and its soldier, wounded in the war. Which war? I don't know. But all the same I can't resist the smiles of the urchins who look after them. Later at Cantho, I heard about a kind of 'ferry racket'. No cripple can just install himself and beg; it's a privilege that must be bought from the ferry men. Even the little girl who sells lottery tickets pays a tax. Yes, indeed—there's a lottery in Vietnam!

I am very proud, because without speaking any Vietnamese, I've made friends. On the ferries, between the cars, the women gather round me, touch me, talk to me. They laugh and I take pictures. Through sign-language, with a lot of understanding and good will, they know all about me by the time we land fifteen minutes later. They know my son, Patrick, for they've studied his photograph— they're surprised that my ears are not pierced and that I don't wear a wedding ring. They also know what my job is; they think I'm very tall, and if they know my age—well, I know theirs, too!

On the outskirts of Tu Duc which was attacked a few days ago, armoured cars have taken up position all along the side of the road. A few soldiers have brought out their camp beds for a nap, others are sheltering from the sun between tanks having a brew-up. Washing is drying almost everywhere, on the tanks, even on the roadside.

A Vietnamese soldier—don't forget that the Americans are not here yet—calmly seated on top of his turret, has turned fisherman, casting his line in the paddy field. There's nonchalance for you! But at night they abandon the area, and leave the road to the Vietcong. Before dusk the tanks regroup and withdraw—to protect the nearest camp!

At Cantho with some French friends—there are only four left there now—I went to a 'new-styled' Vietnamese theatre. If you come back to Vietnam one day and this kind of experience interests you, arm yourself with an aspirin. It's a friendly tip.

It's a Japanese story of the 15th century: a tale of tragic love and the vengeance of the samurais. Loud-speakers, hanging from a length of string and controlled by pulleys, follow the actors as they mouth their lines.

To justify the term 'new-style theatre' there are lots of musical interludes very clearly influenced by 'pop'. The loudspeakers pour out frenzied rhythms at full blast. The hall is full to bursting—three or four children in the same seat. They all react like mad, every new bit of action thrills them. Enormous rats wander all over the place—all part of the show. And it goes on for four hours!

When I came out, the chorus of showmen, the uproar of the traffic, the back-firing Hondas, the flood of music and propaganda from the loudspeakers installed here, as in every town in the province—finished me!

The only relatively quiet time at Cantho is about six or seven in the evening when all the Vietnamese meet beside the Mekong, sitting at tables set out on the quayside, while merchants move among them pushing their carts rich with the smell of hot soup and spices.

Not an American in sight. They are in camp (dinner at six makes the evening interminable) or in their iron-barred billets guarded by M.P.s.

For a few hours Cantho once more belongs to the Vietnamese who stroll about nonchalantly hand in hand or really get down to it. A little later, the advisers gather in one of Madame Quang's night-clubs. This club is not just another Saigon Tea where the girls yawn with boredom. I felt there was something more to it; there's an atmosphere of genuine friendliness, couples become attached to each other, and real emotion enters into it.

Perhaps it's rather like the still-talked-of relationship that used to exist between the boys of the French expeditionary force and the girls of that time. I risk annoying the older generation who never stop pointing out—'Now *we*, in our day . . .' They forget that a mere 125,000 men divided between the north and the south, between Laos and Cambodia, as against 400,000 Americans in South Vietnam alone are two completely different things. It's largely a question of numbers.

But nevertheless, the 7,000 advisers of the Delta manage to get themselves accepted even more successfully. They are not regarded as a body of men against the population, but as individuals. Relations have become more human. Also, because many of the advisers speak, or try to speak, Vietnamese, they are better understood—less despised. The majority of these advisers are against any large-scale occupation by American troops.* This is a bit egotistical, perhaps, for surrounded by such numbers, they'd just be one of a crowd. They'd lose what contact they have with the people and even their relations with the girls would be changed.

I must confess to a special fondness for the West and its colours, its greens and blues, the luminous light, the endless plains. There is also something poignant, arresting, and very sad about this Delta, this great rice field.

'I know what it is,' said Jim Wilde, one of the *Time* correspondents in Paris, who has spent two years in Vietnam, 'it is the end of the great river. The Mekong comes here to die.'

The people are open and obliging; they laugh and joke, they don't nag you with 'Give me five pis (piastres)'. The arrival of an American unit hasn't spoiled them yet. They act naturally.

Before Soc Trang, right in the middle of the road, we ran across a cockfight! Fascinated, I got out of the car, and mingled with the crowd. Everyone was very excited. I couldn't help thinking of General Ky who doesn't need to feel envious of them. Every single Sunday, no matter what's going on—even if it's election day—he spends his morning at Tansonnhut, at the house of one of his air force colonels, taking part in cockfights. Ky has his own stable, and the bets run high. Of course, cockfights are officially prohibited, but that's Vietnam!

When the fight was over, and everyone had calmed down, someone took my hand and invited me to have a bowl of rice and

---

* Three months after I wrote this letter, the entire American Ninth Division landed to take over the area around Mytho.

some hot tea. This was to happen many times. In spite of language difficulties—few of the peasants remember any French—relations were established quickly and simply.

The day before yesterday, just beyond Bac Lien, a coach got stuck in the mud. The driver of another bus announced: 'I'll give you a push.' And he got stuck in his turn. Then the same thing happened to me, and in addition my petrol tank was pierced by a stone. They had to 'carry' the car about fifty yards before they could get it clear of the ruts and see what the damage was. A piece of rag, soap to block the hole, some petrol, and two hours later I was ready to go!

They were shocked because I wanted to pay them, and a little girl brought me more tea, then a napkin and some water to wash my hands.

The place? Right in the middle of Vietcong territory, 500 yards from a village that had been attacked in November; there had been thirty dead among the civilian population. The cockfight, too, was held on the very spot where, eighteen months before, my French friend from Cantho had been taken prisoner. 'They held me for forty-six days,' he told me. 'I was well treated, but not to know what is going to happen is very hard on one's morale.'

At the time I was dying to hear more. Life on 'the other side' fascinated me. But I didn't like to press him.

In fact, I had been skating close to that 'other side' every day, often very close. Perhaps those same peasants, who helped me push the car, are transformed, when night comes, into fierce and determined guerrillas. Perhaps that *nha-qué*, bowing to me over there, was all ready to let off a 'Claymore', a remote-controlled mine? And what about those children, those women? Perhaps they're intelligence agents?

All roads in Vietnam are officially open, but the degree of openness depends on what you are: American, Vietnamese civilian or French. You sense more clearly on the roads than anywhere else the tacit agreement that exists between the people and the N.L.F. (the National Liberation Front).

For example; one day the traffic stopped abruptly—I didn't know why. Five trucks were in front of me, so I got out and went to see. A bench, just an ordinary bench, was barring the way before a bend in the road. One hour later, my patience exhausted, I tried to find out why we had stopped, why the bench was across the road. By drawing on the ground with twigs one of the truck drivers finally managed to explain the situation to me. The bench had been put there by the Vietcong, to let one of their units cross the road beyond the curve, without interruption! Why, I don't know, but about two hours later, without any sign as far as I could see, the driver of the first truck dragged the bench away, and the traffic moved on again!

As I drove along mile after mile, toward the south, I had the impression that the gentlemen's agreement between the Vietcong and the truck drivers was becoming more and more strained, and the number of civilian vehicles that were blown up more and more numerous.

The drivers of the Esso and Shell trucks stop at Bac Lieu. 'Farther on,' they told me, 'that is, from here to Ca Mau, the taxes are too heavy for the business we can do. So we don't deliver beyond this point.' But the water trucks don't belong to the companies, who will not recognize the Vietcong officially. They therefore operate through forwarding agents. It's up to them to pay if they want to—the company washes its hands of them.

The word 'hotel' has long since disappeared from the buildings of Ca Mau. What tourist, even a Vietnamese, would want to venture so far? As for the businessman, whether Chinese, Vietnamese, or French, Ca Mau is in the 'red' zone. Rice paddies, even along the edge of the highroad, are no longer cultivated. The Vietcong are in complete control. Refugees keep pouring in, especially women and children. Are they escaping from the protection of Vietcong or from the bombings? Both, perhaps. Every day, the first becomes more ruthless, the second more intensive. When the refugees come and put themselves under the protection of the local authorities, the government allots each family 3,000 piastres on arrival, and then thirty piastres a day after that. But Saigon has no illusions. Brothers, husbands, cousins or uncles have remained on 'the other side'. And one way or another, the refugees continue to send information back to the 'Viets'.

If I had trouble finding a hotel, I also had trouble finding the M.A.C.V., the camp of the Vietnamese and their American advisers. Finally I stopped a jeep. After gaping at me for five minutes, the sergeant managed to speak.

'Would you believe it! A girl, a female reporter, here in Ca Mau! Coming by car, alone. And without grenade or pistol. Only with a smile! My God, I must be dreaming!'

I was offered the room of Colonel Blake, who was at Vangtau. 'A free half-day for everyone in honour of Michèle,' announced Major Conley.

One of the officers told me in a trembling voice, 'It's more than six months since I've shaken hands with a lady!'

Opening the wrong door I almost fell over backwards! Crates of beer from floor to ceiling and right to the end of an enormous room! It made me dizzy!

'Oh, yes! Seven truck loads of beer! Seven thousand dollars' worth!'

That evening the Americans—all 'good guys'—tried by songs, charades, and poems that I didn't understand at all, to recapture the spirit of their college days. Leaning on his cane, the representative of the U.S.O.M.* was the only one to stay quiet. He was content to smile as he watched his countrymen trying to forget the war, Vietnam, and their own problems.

He talked to me of the charcoal which is impossible to get at in the heart of Vietcong territory. Of Song Ong Doc, where fish that is sent direct to Singapore is paid for in currency in Saigon. The headland of Ca Mau was the rice granary of the Delta, the most productive province, even if the rice was not of the best quality. 'And because the rice fields belong to the Vietcong, and all normal life is impossible with the continual bombing,' he told me, 'we are trying, and the Government is trying, to turn the peasants into artisans.'

I was just hearing from him that there were three doctors at Ca Mau—but no nurse because it was 'too dangerous for a woman', when the Vietnamese Lieutenant Duc interrupted us. Although it was midnight, he insisted on telling me about his studies at the French lycée in Dalat, about Victor Hugo, and about some poems dedicated to his daughter Pauline, who was drowned in a pond.

I was sorry to leave without seeing Father Hon, the Chinese missionary who operates in the territory of Ha Yen with a number of Nung soldiers under his command. A former captain in Chiang

* United States Operation Mission—an organization which distributes American Civil Aid.

Kai-shek's army, he is the principal figure in the southernmost province of the west.

As I promised, I'll write to you at each important stage of my 'journey across Vietnam'. It is more fun than keeping a diary. Put up a map in your house, stick pins in it, and teach your son geography!

I forgot to tell you that an American magazine would like the logbook of my journey. But after all, I haven't really begun the journey yet. Isn't Ca Mau my starting point?

Love.

8

A Mine explodes in front of my Car

Saigon, December 18, 1966
My dear Pat,
   Though I haven't been blown up by a mine yet, I did nearly get myself killed.
   I left Ca Mau in rain and wind: the rice fields were empty, there was no one on the road, and even the villages were almost deserted. As Eugène* would have said, 'It smells of Vietcong round here!'
   The best solution in a situation like that; jam your foot on the acclerator! Bullets whistled past me, but—No!—I was not the target of four Vietcong, but instead four members of the 'Home Guard', amusing themselves. Their laughing faces, reflected in my mirror, threw me into a helpless rage. I saw them dig each other in the ribs as they continued to take aim. I thought of the advice my journalist friends had given me before I left: 'The ones to fear most are not the disciplined Vietcong, but the Home Guard or the Government troops who are always on the lookout for a scrap.'
   Do you know that these famous village militias have joined forces on several occasions with the N.L.F. soldiers to take a crack at the American camps?
   A certain amount of traffic gives me confidence that the 'gentlemen's agreement' between the transport drivers and the Vietcong is still working, but this deserted road had me worried. Had the Vietcong stopped all traffic that day, as they sometimes did? It was possible, but as the grapevine functions in Vietnamese, I was ignorant of it, and so found myself driving all alone. To make matters worse—was it bad luck or thoughtlessness?—the car was loaded with crates of beer, letters, and packages for the two American advisers in that Godforsaken spot, Gia Ria.
   It was with a sigh of relief that I finally reached it. Gia Ria had

* Eugène Mannoni, of *France-Soir*.

FH

been attacked the night before, and I was a welcome visitor, a kind of Santa Claus with my packages for Major Pilaud and Captain MacGee.

'Do you know what was in those black cylinders?' Pilaud asked me. 'Secret documents!' I came out in a delayed cold sweat. Had I been stopped I would undoubtedly have been taken for a spy! And I didn't fancy being kept in a cage! Just two days before, a missionary had told me that it is in the Ca Mau area that the Delta Vietcong keep the few American prisoners who fall into their hands. 'Shut in bamboo cages, they are paraded from one village in the peninsula to another. In each new place they are tried and sentenced to death. After they have publicly repented the sentence is suspended until they reach the next village where the same farce begins again.'

I decided to take the longest route back to Cantho, to make a complete circuit of the Delta. Between Long Xuyen and Rach Gia the road runs parallel with a canal. On a strip of ground about three feet wide between the canal and the road refugees were living in straw huts. They had fled from the Vietcong because their fields had been bombed, and also because their rice paddies had been flooded by a recent rise in the level of the Mekong. All light had gone out of their eyes. There are no longer outstretched hands and invitations to share the family tea, but resignation and indifference.

At Rach Gia, both officials and military are preoccupied with two problems: defectors from the Vietcong or *chieu hois* (open arms), and the latest American bombardment. The setting: three hills running down to the sea-shore—nicknamed the Three Sisters—and a church.

'The church was used as a political school,' the American adviser explained. 'We dropped rockets and bombs all round the outside. But the minute they came out and tried to escape, we dropped leaflets instead, saying 'Come over to our side'.

'Were they all partisans?'

'No, there were women, children, and peasants, too. They're under our protection now. You'll see them in the refugee camp at Kien Luong.'

What else could they have done?

'The three hills were cleaned up?' I went on asking questions.

'No! The partisans hung on and are still in possession.'
'How many are they?'
'About fifteen. But a squad of Vietcong is worth a whole battalion of our Government troops. We keep strafing them and dropping leaflets.'

One of those pilots, during his briefing back in Saigon, will have the nerve to give an account of *his* bombardment, as excited as though he'd arranged a magnificent display of fireworks.

Several days later, his pals will still be talking about it—it's sickening!

As for the *chieu hois*—the defectors—they are the pride and joy of the civil aid officers. It made me sick to see one of them, in all good faith, going to endless trouble to please 'his' converts. But what is to stop the simple peasant who is starving from pretending to be an ex-Vietcong? In a flash of enlightenment, the officer admitted: 'We must take care not to overdo it to the point of annoying the rest of the population.'

I questioned some of the defectors. Naturally not one of them had been a guerrilla or had soiled his hands with a gun! The words grenade and mine meant nothing to them. They had all been concerned exclusively with 'propaganda'. Exasperated, I finally asked: 'Is there one single person in your group who has, even for one day, been a real guerrilla?'

'Ask the camp leader. He ought to know,' were the last words the interpreter translated for me. Some of them couldn't have cared less about me, the Americans or the Government—which doesn't surprise me—and will go on passing information, and go back to the 'other side' as soon as they have put on a bit of weight. Or else they really have deserted, in which case the Vietcong have not lost anything!

At the former Residence, I lunched with the head of the province, the commander of the Seventh South Vietnamese division, General Thi, and his adviser, Colonel Bingham. No local dishes, but a bouillabaisse.

'Rach Gia is famous for the best bouillabaisse in all Vietnam, a recipe from Marseilles,' Thi explained.

As the road had been cut, they took me by helicopter to Ha Tien on the Cambodian frontier.

According to *Time* magazine, Ha Tien is eighty per cent under

Vietcong control. Six miles out the Seven Hills are certainly a favourite zone for the B-52 napalm raids. But here on the frontier, all was quiet.

There were no longer rice fields, but savannahs, palm trees, and coconuts. The population is mostly Khmer. No more concerts of hooting car horns, loudspeakers, and propaganda. Instead tarred streets, gardens and houses covered with flaming bougainvillaeas. Not a car, only pedicabs and Buddhists in saffron-coloured robes. . . . It was a long time since I'd experienced such a feeling of peace.

Down at the harbour, women were peacefully mending fishing nets. In the shops, here, there and everywhere, was tortoise-shell.

"All the tortoise-shell in Vietnam comes from here,' General Thi told me as he presented me with a fan, 'For your evenings at the opera!'

At the back of the shops the tortoises are kept in different tanks according to their size. The chiselling and polishing is done in adjoining rooms.

There is only one hotel, where employees of the R.M.K.* in Rach Gia come for weekends. I envy them! It seems like paradise, and very far from the war.

Before leaving, Captain Smith of the Special Forces said to me, 'Our operations are quiet and undramatic . . . just one or two Vietcong from time to time.'

Was he dissatisfied or pleased?

Long Xuyen and Chau Doc, provinces of Hoa Hoa, are also the two quietest provinces in the Delta. I am not the only person besides the Vietnamese on the roads for I passed some Land-Rovers of American civilians.

At Chau Doc I saw the 'official' reconciliation between the Buddhists and the Moslems!

Canoe races on the river, gaudy costumes, music, songs, a reception at the mosque. Barefooted, legs crossed underneath me, I felt I was no longer in Vietnam, but in some other part of the Far East.

'As soon as we engage the Vietcong, they've got less than a mile to go—then, whoops!—they're on the other side of the frontier, in

* Coalition of American public companies with exclusive rights to all work done in Vietnam for the American forces.

safety!' said Colonel Brewer, of the Special Forces, also in his socks, with legs crossed. 'If you want to see some action, your best plan is to make a film of the volleyball match!'

However, during the night the Vietcong provided the action: two civilians kidnapped, another with his throat cut.

I tried to see the Vietnamese sergeant who, after taking a year to get himself transferred to Saigon—because of serious family troubles —still could not leave Chau Doc: he hadn't enough money to pay the 'separation tax' to his superior. His wife had given me a package for him, but he had gone off on an exercise for four days.

At Long Xuyen, as I was sitting down to a Chinese soup—and quite ready to eat far too much of it—I was suddenly surrounded by a group of girl students, unmistakable in their white tunics.

'You are French. We're studying French in school. Can we sit down?'

They all wanted to talk at the same time. Young, pretty, smiling, they were bubbling with life. They made me tell them about Paris, about France. Their only desire was to get away, to leave Vietnam. They dreamed of being air hostesses, as Mme. Ky had been. But when I made a comment—not very tactful, perhaps—about the 'girls' of Saigon, one of the students reacted violently. 'Instead of criticizing,' she burst out, 'why don't you try to understand? There are families where one girl—and it's often the eldest—has to sacrifice herself to keep the rest of the household alive. And because the family tie is very strong, she finds that quite normal. My sister is one of those 'dutiful ones' at Cantho. I am not ashamed of it, I'm proud of it. There are nine of us at home and my father has . . . disappeared.'

Sixteen or seventeen years old, and quite sturdy, with two long plaits down her back, she had laughing eyes and mouth, and a determined chin. I spent the night at her place, in a tiny room which opened on the street, with five of us—some of her brothers and sisters—all packed in together. We talked until one in the morning. She denied that she was Communist, but 'fiercely nationalist, which explains why I'm anti-American!' She was furious about the local authorities 'who taunt us with their cars, their comfort, and their money. We all pay taxes to the Vietcong, but at least we know that they won't fill their own pockets.'

In the glove compartment of my car the next morning I found a drawing—peasants in a rice field, with the inscription: 'To Michèle, whom I trust.'

At Sadec, headquarters of the seventh division, they were all getting ready for the inevitable party in my honour. The umpteenth since I left Saigon!

It is always difficult to be the only woman in a camp. You can be killed by kindness. Sometimes I wanted to be alone, not talking. . . . But how could I refuse and go calmly off to bed at nine o'clock in the evening? They'd be hurt, they wouldn't understand.

That night, as Commander Williams of the Navy had given me permission, I preferred to go out on patrol—twelve hours on the Bassac River.

The River Patrol Boats plough along the river, two by two, twenty-four hours out of twenty-four. They carry a machine-gun in the bow, another at the stern, three American officers and a Vietnamese policeman. Their job: to inspect all craft, including junks—their cargo and their ship's papers. At night there is a curfew for all river traffic, except transports for the sick and wounded.

The Vietnamese policeman, and he alone, has the right to board a junk, search the interior, and examine the papers. The pass written in Vietnamese is in any case incomprehensible to the Americans. There has to be complete trust between the naval officers and the Vietnamese police; otherwise, a company or an entire regiment of armed Vietcong could pass right under their noses. The whole thing would then become a farce. Just one or two Vietcong agents among those inspectors would be enough to . . .

About one o'clock in the morning, an alert . . . we were fired at (nothing to protect us, no shelter, we were an ideal target).

If I had to produce one single picture to explain Vietnam, it might be this: while the Viets were firing on us from across the river, a transistor radio poured out floods of rock-and-roll which came to us in waves between the burst of gunfire.

In spite of a whole day on the road and twelve hours of patrol duty without sleeping, I set out the following morning feeling surprisingly fresh. As I was driving along the road I met a Buddhist funeral procession and, at the insistence of the relatives and friends of the dead, I stopped. Cakes and tea, followed by a pantomime in my honour! Once again I was touched and fascinated by the simplicity of it all. Not once in the last four months had I managed to make such direct and natural contact with the people. Now, more than ever, I was glad that I'd undertaken 'my crazy trip'. It seemed to me that I was at last beginning to put my finger on the real face of Vietnam and its inhabitants. And I realized that they had charmed me, and that I loved them.

I turned back towards Saigon. As there were no vegetables in the market, it dawned on me that the road from Dalat was cut. No matter; while I was waiting I would go to Tay Ninh, near the Cambodian border. It was there, three weeks before, that I had taken part in Operation Attleboro, the most important action of the war to date.

This time there were no tents, no dinner with General Dupuy, and none of the 500 V.C. mortar shells of the last day of Operation Attleboro. All I found there was a French rubber plantation.

Although the manager taught me a lesson, he also surprised me, considering the generally narrow-minded outlook of the French colony:

'Why do you wander about with the French flag in full view at the front and back of your car?' he asked. 'If it's because of a mine or a sniper, it's a useless protection. If you are stopped by the Vietcong, your passport will carry more weight than the tri-colour on your number-plate. The advantages are therefore nil. But you came here over a road held and guarded by the Americans, with American tanks at every crossroad. Do you know what your flag means to them? "I am a Frenchwoman, and I thumb my nose at you!" You are brave—try and show a bit of breeding, too!'

My ego took a bad beating!

He lives with his wife right on the plantation in conditions of the greatest nervous strain: tanks, G.I.s, and Vietcong follow each other through the rubber trees. . . . The bombing never stops.

'During Operation Attleboro,' they told me, 'we had to lock our doors. Every time there was an explosion, they'd all fly open with a bang. And the Americans still hold a grudge against us for surviving!'

All through drinks and dinner they were perfectly calm, talking of one thing and another . . . while gunfire was raging only fifty yards away. 'Don't worry,' they ended by saying, 'the Home Guard must have come face to face with the Vietcong, by mistake!' Later,

sensing my blatant curiosity, he told me the news: 'Two Home
Guard dead, killed by one of their own men, who thought he was
up against the Vietcong!'

Here the grotesque reigns supreme!

The next day the manager gave me a guide to visit the Caodaist
temple at Tayninh.

A fusing of three religions, or rather, three philosophies—
Buddhism, Taoism, Confucianism, not to mention Victor Hugo!—
Caodaism was founded in 1926 by Ngô Van Chrên and officials of
the French colonial service. The 'spiritual father' is Ly Tai Pé.

Priests in saffron-yellow, sky-blue, or reddish-purple robes pass
before the portrait of Victor Hugo, 'the great French poet, recognized by his own revelation as one of the spirits of the white lodge
under the name of Nguyet Tam Chau Nhon'. Farther on, a statue
of Joan of Arc in a prominent place. And eyes, or rather 'the eye',
is reproduced everywhere: on columns, in stained-glass windows,
to right and to left, on the ceiling, on the ground. The eye is everywhere! I felt as if I were Cain.

> The eye moves the heart,
> Sovereign master of visual perception,
> Visual perception derives from the principle of intelligence,
> Intelligence derives from the divine,
> The divine Principle—is I myself.

There were columns of gaudy stucco—I have never seen a temple
in such bad taste. I must confess that in spite of my guide's speeches
and explanations, I know just as little about the Caodaists as I did
before.

Though there is still a road to Pnom Penh, one can no longer go
by car to Sihanouk's palace. Road-blocks of barbed wire stop all
traffic before the Cambodian frontier.

That day I was not interested in Cambodia, but in the market
that had been set up on the border between the two countries.
Walking along the embankments, I passed dozens of Vietnamese
trotting along, pushing bicycles overloaded with all sorts of extra-
ordinary goods. They were making for a wooden shanty-town built
right in the middle of a rice field. I suddenly felt I was back in the
Beauce region with its flat sombre countryside and its low clouds.
I was in mud up to my knees.

On an operation with a unit of the First Infantry Division, at the Cambodian frontier. (*Reporters Associés*)

At Da Nang, I take off in a C.30 with Pierre Schoendoerffer's team.
War is also hours of waiting. (*Reporters Associés*)

One woman's enough—on my account, they shave every day.

(*Reporters Associés*)

Somewhere in the Binh Dinh area, with the First Cavalry Division.

(Reporters Associés)

With Pat Schoendoerffer, between Pleiku and An Khê: after the ambush.

This market has everything: Vietnamese and Cambodian products, of course, but it is also an off-shoot of the American P.X. in Saigon, and there are French goods as well—books of elementary mathematics, Evian water, and 'Miss Dior' toilet water. Goods from Communist China—by what devious route had they reached here? —lay alongside goods from Nationalist China! The police had given me special permission to visit the market but had forbidden me to take pictures. After seeing it, I could understand why.

On the way back it took me twelve hours to drive fifty miles. I met two American convoys coming from Cuchi, the base of the 25th division. Names to haunt your dreams: Cuchi Express, Orient Express! Headlights blazing and at full speed they passed, with helmets and bulletproof jackets, eyes riveted to the road, the drivers looked like motorists of the Gay Nineties. The G.I. beside each driver carried his M-16 in one hand and tossed sweets with the other. At every cross-road, and on both ends of each bridge, tanks mounted guard.

Just short of Cuchi an explosion? Fifty yards in front of me: a mine!

Was it a delayed explosion meant to catch the last of the American trucks, or, on the other hand . . . had it gone off too soon? Was it meant for me? I don't know, but fortunately no one was hurt. Only, for me, a crack in the windscreen and a great fright!

In Saigon the Renault manager welcomed me back with: 'In spite of the agreement with Paris, I'm going to take the car back You've given me white hairs, and cold sweats!'

I kept the car. . . .

9

The Viets miss a Rendezvous

Nha Trang, December 24, 1966
My dear Pat,
Once again vegetables appeared in the Saigon market. The rains had carried a bridge away, apparently—but now I could get on with my journey. My plan was to strike out at random, take the road to Dalat, and see the Vietcong at close quarters for the first time: just tax-collectors, some of them—who lack charm in every country in the world—but soldiers, too, and N.L.F. soldiers, at that.

Of course, up till now the French had never had any trouble, and had always got through without difficulty, but you never know! To be on the safe side I prepared an emergency kit, in case for some unknown reason I had to make a little stay in the mountains! But I was too lucky—or if you prefer it, not lucky enough—for the Vietcong who are usually there for 365 days out of 365 did not show up at the rendezvous! An engagement with Government troops in the morning caused them to absent themselves for a few hours! But I'm going too fast. Let's begin at the beginning with the motorway to Bien Hoa.

I don't believe that there's a more dangerous road in all Vietnam than this motorway, built by the Americans four years ago. You risk a collision, if not a more serious accident at every moment— grenades, mines, snipers, an ambush—and all within ten miles of Saigon. Heavy traffic, convoys one after the other, civilian trucks, public transport, cars, motorcycles, Hondas—all rush by on the right, on the left, or in the middle of the highway. From time to time there's an explosion: a grenade destroys a military vehicle. Gunfire at dawn or at nightfall: it's an ambush that lets loose an avalanche of aeroplanes.

The G.I.s or the A.R.V.N.* go into action two yards from the macadam: they advance at the double, camouflaging themselves

* A.R.V.N.: Army of the Republic of (South) Vietnam.

in the bushes. A little farther on, some Vietnamese protected by armed guards, fill thousands of sand-bags, chattering and laughing as they do so. And finally there's an enormous pile of stuff, equipment of every kind covering several square miles, an area that grows larger daily—hundreds of jeeps, hundreds of guns of all sizes, trucks, and whole rows of crates not yet opened.

In camp, protected by barbed wire and guarded by M.P.s, the G.I.s are hard at work erecting small huts and prefabricated latrines. They need them, too!

The incessant roar of the jets as they take off and land at Tan Son Nhut or Bien Hoa. . . . F.100s or C.130s which are shot down from time to time by a sniper lurking near by . . . nothing reminds you more of the war, of the numbers and power of the Americans than those ten miles of highroad leading from the gates of Saigon. It also reminds you of the Vietcong, whose presence you can smell at every turn.

Sometimes you come across an oasis of peace—who knows why— where the Vietnamese fish peacefully in the paddy fields.

At the end of the motorway, the Catholic villages begin, peopled by refugees from the north. Crowds of churches stand side by side— there are 350 of them. The Tonkinese have rebuilt their communities exactly as they used to be in the northern dioceses round Phat Diem or Bui Chou, district by district, laid out in the same relationship to the clock-tower which itself was as near a likeness as possible to the one they had left behind. They've even brought the bells with them. In one of these villages, a toothless Frenchwoman had been living the Vietnamese life as a Vietnamese for the past forty years.

Then came a police checkpoint: that's where the truck-drivers, squeezed like a lemon by both sides, must pay the first of many taxes. Here they check the goods being carried, and search the trucks for weapons. If the 'tip' is not generous enough, 'they' can always find an excuse, and make the drivers wait for several days, the contents of their trucks spread out on the road, 'pending a more thorough investigation'.

Here, no receipts were given: the deal was 'under the counter'.

Some seventy miles out, I stopped for some Chinese soup 'chez Robert'.

'I haven't seen a Frenchman for four months,' he told me. 'If they stop you, don't on any account speak English, even if they open the conversation in that language. But you'll never be able to get through with your car! There are holes in the road where trucks disappear completely!'

He was not exaggerating.

On that Saigon–Dalat road, the Vietcong hold, among other things, the Banana-Tree Pass—a thirty-mile stretch. The Government Water and Forestry Service has obviously not been able to venture into this area, and the last rains have deepened and enlarged the ruts and craters. It took me eight hours to drive twenty-one miles. Though N.L.F. soldiers hold the Pass, Government troops are immediately behind and ahead of them. I met several groups, and invariably they swaggered like conquerors as they posed before my camera.

True warriors!

Some of the drivers spoke a little French, and as there were frequent traffic jams, we had a chance to talk. Their unanimous opinion: 'Vietminh, nothing say to French,' but in spite of this, 'You are brave, because one never knows what might happen!' No private cars, only trucks and overloaded buses. Without the friendly help of all these people I would have come to a sticky end in the bottom of a hole. But they had everything necessary to help me—shovels and tow-ropes—and plenty of practice!

Over the worst stretches, the passengers get out of the bus, and join it again farther on. The trucks, however, don't unload: at all costs, they must get through. Some of them are lucky; others, if the differential or a half-shaft goes, sometimes have to wait for more than ten days for the new part to be brought from Saigon by a mate who might break down himself several miles farther on. Impassive and phlegmatic, they settle down beside the road, eating and sleeping in or under the truck, which becomes their home for the time being. When that happens, do the Vietcong collect a visitor's tax? I wonder.

'We pay between five and ten per cent,' one driver told me, 'depending upon the value of the load we're carrying or the price of the freight tickets. Or sometimes a lump sum. Between the Government toll-gates and those of the Vietcong on the Saigon–Qui Nhon road we may pay up to 40,000 piastres a load. The Vietcong give us a receipt for each payment. We're not afraid of the Vietcong

—they play fair if we do, too. But there are bandits or 'cowboys'—gangs of looters with long hair who seize you for ransom, steal, and kill. They're armed with grenades, and knives, and with them there's no question of a receipt or a discussion. Be careful just after Blao—that's their favourite spot—especially a woman alone. Join and stick close to a group of truckers. The Vietcong aren't there today! You're in luck! You'll see the truck drivers wave their hands: that means "All clear." If they signal one, two, or three—that means: 'They are one, two, or three miles up the road.'

In every country where communications are difficult people are inclined to help each other. Here, the bonds uniting the drivers are specially strong, for on top of the bad roads there are taxes, mines and bandits. Because I was taking the same risks as the drivers, they adopted me. I felt as if I'd joined a brotherhood. And up to a point, I felt protected.

And where were the Americans, you ask me? There are only 450 at Dalat, and a few advisers at Blao or Djirring: this is not an operational sector for American divisions.

Farther along the road, I came across a stalled Land-Rover with its clutch burned out. I picked up the driver in my Dauphine. Driving 'à deux' was easier. He would get out, remove large stones, guide the wheels. Often we passed the edge of a hole with a truck stuck in it, then our roofs would be on the same level! Once again my petrol tank was pierced by a stone, but now I'm an expert: a bit of rag, some soap, more petrol . . . and we're off again! My passenger, who spoke fluent French, was a native of Huê. His grandmother was Bao Dai's aunt. But I have never yet met a Vietnamese from Huê who was not more or less connected with the imperial family. He told me that he was an apiarist and that although he was anti-American, he was pro-French.

'The French have a civilization. They are better company. They married Vietnamese girls. Conversation with Americans is impossible. We feel closer to the French. We are the Latins of the Far East.'

'You were in the French army during the war?'

The 'No, I was Vietminh!' was said with such violence that I jumped.

'Why aren't you Vietcong now?'

'Ill-health. I couldn't stay in the mountains more than three years. The diet of rice and salt was too hard on me. But my sympathies are still with them. After a fashion I help them.'

What could he have meant? Did he keep them supplied with honey? But he preferred to change the conversation.

'Is virginity very important in France?

'. . . !'

'In Vietnam it is—especially in the mountains. On the wedding day the families wait for the report; if the husband has been cheated with his "goods", there must be compensation—usually, buffaloes!'

In Blao curfew is at eight o'clock. It was five to eight before I finally found the French plantation. That whole area is mostly inhabited by 'Moi', who have been resettled in villages bordering the highroad. The mountains belong to the Vietcong, who therefore control the roads as well.

There, sandwiched between the threat of the Vietcong and the American advisers an entire family is trying to survive. Though they are French they are also Alsatians, and everything reminds you of it: the architecture of their wooden house, its furnishings and engravings. The little boat at the edge of the swimming pool is called *Strasbourg*.

Michèle, the eldest daughter, is eighteen, Christian nine, and Sophie seven. Their mother teaches them from textbooks provided by the Universal School. The father came here in 1932. He has developed the whole place himself, built everything with his own hands: the house, the swimming pool, a landing strip, the plantation itself. The children, born in Dalat, speak both mountain dialect and American fluently. I can understand why it is hard for them—for him especially—to leave Vietnam. Their house, their plantation, is a sort of no-man's-land. I can easily believe that he is the only planter who does not pay taxes to the Vietcong, while at the same time trying to remain independent of the Americans.

'*They* have requisitioned the landing strip, but the Vietcong know that I don't take any pay for it. *They* are building a bigger one in the direction of the Special Forces camp; but though it's not finished, it's already been attacked three times by mortar fire. Mine is better protected. The Vietcong dropped leaflets saying that they'd be in Blao by Christmas. So a regiment of the A.R.V.N.* arrived from Ban Me Thuot two days ago.'

* Army of the Republic of Vietnam.

'I counted 198 trucks,' said Christian.

'Since their arrival I can sleep more peacefully,' Madame continued. 'There are 3,000 Vietcong in the mountains.'

'I want to go back to France,' complained Christian. 'War's no fun. In France they have everything. . . .' And he added with a rush: 'There are even harvesting machines! And then I have friends in France. They all want to play at war . . . but I don't like to.' He wanted to be a pilot when he grew up, but not in the army. 'I don't want to be killed by a bullet.' Two days before, from her terrace, Madame watched through binoculars while an American reconnaissance plane was shot down by a tank that had just been captured by the Vietcong.

'They waved their hands wildly, and the bursts of gunfire came at the same time.'

That night, falling in with the custom of the household, I slept with my door unlocked. The next day, as they do every morning, Sophie and Christian made their tour of the runway in a plane, an F.A.C., without leaving the ground. The American pilots and advisers are crazy about these two fair-haired children who remind them of their own kids. Each feels reassured by the presence of the others—a touch of human warmth in the midst of war. I left the family, moved by their hospitality but heavy-hearted, too. They survive! Yes, but at what a price! And for how much longer? They are at the end of their tether and their courage rouses all my sympathy.

'You should have been here last evening! Lang, the tax-collector for the Home Guard, made his three-monthly visit.'

So said another Frenchman, a small planter. In these parts there is nothing glamorous about the word plantation. They have just enough money to live from day to day, and they have not set foot in France for more than ten years. 'Here, look at this receipt: 5,000 piastres every quarter. It's difficult to argue about it, to say "No, only 3,000". If you refuse they ship you home and that's even more expensive. Mind you, taking a trip with them can be amusing. But paying 50,000 piastres to buy your freedom again makes it an expensive holiday! You could go to Hong Kong for the same price, and the food would be even better!'

After almost thirty years in Vietnam he has seen other wars, and his morale can hold out against anything.

'Why should I hide the fact that I pay taxes to the Vietcong? If I don't, I'd be kidnapped, for a ransom I could never pay. The Government knows it, just as they know that they can't protect me. So I pay up! That doesn't mean I am anti-American. The French used to pay taxes to the Vietminh, and in Algeria to the N.L.F.'

I left them, rather late, and had a breakdown, alone on the road, several miles from Dalat. To plug a hole in the petrol tank I had put in too much soap and this had got into the carburettor and blocked it. As I had no torch, there was nothing I could do but prepare to spend a night on the road with the risk of being picked up or shot down by the Vietcong or those famous bandits. The Vietnamese who got me moving again two hours later had neither hives nor bees, but a rose-garden in Dalat.

'It was incredibly lucky for you that I was late, too,' he said. 'After nine o'clock at night no one risks the road. We'll have to tow the car, otherwise you'll never find it again. The Vietcong will begin by stripping it tonight, and the Government troops will finish the job tomorrow morning.'

Dalat is a corner of Europe in the middle of Vietnam. There's a lake, mountains, pine trees, waterfalls, houses with chimneys, wood fires. Vegetables, too—150 tons of them and half are flown out daily to the American units in the field. There are flowers—1,500 roses a day and a French school—the students are all over the city. There is also a military academy, the Vietnamese war college, where the parades are as good as West Point, though the military instruction is not on the same level.

Dalat is out of bounds to Americans, except for the 450 who are stationed there. Perhaps the best way to describe Dalat is these two stories:

The vegetable growers wanted to blow up a bridge, to cut the road and make prices rise. . . . Consequently the Vietcong had to put guards on the bridges near Dalat in order to keep open an important source of revenue.

As for the second story, it takes place at the lodgings of the military academy advisers—a magnificent villa which once belonged to Bao-Dai's concubine. There is no camp at Dalat, all the Americans are scattered about in such villas. Log-fires, hi-fi music, dinner by candlelight. One of the colonels drew me over to the window and said,

'Look at Dalat: this is not war. There in the mountains all around us—that's where the war begins. Tonight, as I came home,' he went on, 'I caught the Vietnamese M.P. asleep at his post. I shook him. "Listen, what if the Vietcong arrive!" He looked at me and smiled. "No Vietcong Dalat, Colonel!" '

There you have it. There is no war at Dalat, only advisers who are dying of boredom and who try to occupy themselves by organizing visits for cadets in the various American divisions!

'The First Cavalry Division boys,' Colonel Green told me, 'were given a magnificent briefing followed by a visit to the front. Sixty-six men came the first day, forty-nine the next day, and twenty-four the third; the rest all reported sick!' The advisers were disillusioned and made no further effort. They preferred to get on with their enormous abstract made of cuttings from *Playboy*.

In the mountains between Dalat and Phan Rang the train sometimes runs beside the road through the pine-woods, one of the few main line trains still working. It is not exactly a Pullman service but a wheezy engine drawing old wooden goods trucks. At Duong-Duong, the 'Seabees'—the Marine engineers—were building a market. The dam itself was built by the Japanese, as part of their war indemnity.

But this was not my lucky day. After I had been taken for an American by the Vietnamese, the American captain refused to let me into the camp. Perhaps because I was French?

There are so many hold-ups that I no longer worry about them. I've become almost as stolid as a Vietnamese!

As usual, we managed to talk sign language, and as usual, they surrounded and touched me. The heat was unbearable: a woman dipped her handkerchief in the stream and gave it to me. But when I came back to my car, after talking with the G.I.s in the convoy that was blocking the road—a trailer had two wheels in the ditch—all the Vietnamese turned their backs on me, or to be exact, ignored me completely. You remember the Vietnamese when they don't want to see you, that vacant expression in their eyes!

Because I had stayed so long talking to the G.I.s, they felt that I was American, or at least very 'pro-American', so I didn't interest them any more and they ignored me.

By the time we'd been held up for six hours, night had fallen and it was too late to go on to Phan Rang without running considerable risks. The roads, at night, belong to the Vietcong, and one of the elementary security rules is *never, on any account, travel at night*.

But nevertheless: 'No civilians allowed in camp!'

Although the captain of the convoy had expressly ordered me to stop, and on no account travel at night, although the village was quite unsafe and I had asked for his 'assistance', although as a last resort I showed my press card, nothing could make the American military adviser change his mind. He kept repeating, 'No civilians in the camp!'

I was on the point of going on to Phan Rang in spite of the many risks that it entailed when the Vietnamese commander hurried up, flung wide the gates of the camp for me, and put his lodgings at my disposal. Though at last I had a place to spend the night, I was furious with the American captain who had just had his nose put out of joint by the Vietnamese commander he was 'advising'. The latter, on the other hand, was not sorry to be able to give the American a lesson!

Phan Rang, Camranh Bay, Nha Trang: the road between these places is open to Americans—at least a civilian jeep is allowed to go through unescorted. Camranh Bay is one of the most beautiful natural harbours in the world. Both the French and the Japanese made use of it, and now the Americans want to make it another Singapore or Okinawa. Among the dunes they have set up the largest supply base in Vietnam to relieve the permanent congestion in Saigon. Everything is prefabricated: the runway for jets, as well as the floating landing-stage which was brought by sea from South Carolina. Camranh, the safest anchorage in Vietnam, represents millions of dollars' worth of figures and planning. It was there that Johnson chose to land while we were all waiting for him at Danang.

I had often flown over Camranh and had promised myself that I'd go there. But the torrential rains put me off making the detour.

I had always heard people say that Nha Trang was one of the most beautiful bays in Vietnam with a marvellous beach, and villas on the cliffs—a sort of Vietnamese Cannes! But that Nha Trang no longer exists. The most beautiful of anchorages is invaded by warships, and the beach by oil; the villas are requisitioned by the army, and the famous coast road is nothing but holes, jeeps, trucks, and military convoys.

Saigon, by comparison, seems a haven of peace. Its reputation as the capital of vice is a myth; in my opinion, Nha Trang wins that title. The pretence of discretion which, after all, is kept up in Saigon, does not exist here, where flirting begins openly in the streets, and in fact all over the place, and where the beach is the favourite setting for lovers to come to grips!

The French embassy has a villa here, completely over-grown by grass, but it is already occupied. I was welcomed eagerly by the head of the P.I.O.* who was delighted to put a villa at my disposal, a press centre where no one ever comes. Nha Trang, the supply base, is of no interest to the correspondents who are looking for 'war', for action.

I dined with a journalist who had come to interview Billy Graham. We were taken for a ride by some local Frenchmen, more money-grabbing than usual, who run a restaurant.

It's eight o'clock now, and I'm already back in my room. It's Christmas Eve and it's also the truce. But for me Christmas tomorrow means Ninh Hoa and to Ban Me Thuot, the Vietcong tax . . . the unknown.

Happy Christmas to you all!

* Press Information Office.

10

Ears and Nose

Kontum, 2, January 1967

Good morning.

Christmas with the Vietcong, New Year's Eve with lepers!

I could think of a better way to spend the holidays, but it is really not so bad—at least from the point of view of the unusual!

I think I shall leave the Vietcong till later—in spite of your impatience to 'know all'—and tell you first about Kontum, the Mountain people, Sister Marie-Louise, and Pat Smith.

Kontum is in some ways a haven of peace. No guns, no jets. Not too hot, either: we are 1,600 feet up, I think. Every day, or almost every day, there are hundreds of coloured parachutes in the sky: men of the 101st Airborne Division on training jumps.

A year ago this was one of the most threatened towns in South Vietnam—if not the most. The Vietcong surrounded it—they are only two or three miles away, at most. Now convoys to Pleiku run daily, and two jeeps can even venture out together without escort. On the road northwards to Dakto, military convoys are rare, but civilian traffic makes use of it, particularly two unusual women with powerful personalities, who have made Kontum their property.

'Are you going to visit my two tigresses?' Monsignor Seiltz asked me with a laugh as we stood in the Archbishop's palace, a large Normandy-style house covered with bougainvillaea.

The first of the 'tigresses' is Dr. Patricia Marie Smith. Arriving in the highlands in 1959, she began by working at Sister Marie-Louise's leper hospital. Such an arrangement couldn't possibly last for long!

Starting with a dispensary and five beds in the provincial hospital, she now runs the hospital at Minh Quy which she has built up entirely with funds supplied by Catholic societies.

'Forty beds for 120 patients! We've got to go on enlarging! Fortunately, most of the patients would rather sleep on mattresses on the ground, or even under the veranda. Having a patient means that we have some of his family living and eating here, too. We have kitchens, but many of the patients do their own cooking. We leave them to it.'

Fifteen months ago, when Kontum was surrounded and almost captured by the Vietcong, the military authorities begged her to leave her hospital.

'It's outside the town! You'll be the first hit!'

'Don't be ridiculous. How can I leave my patients?' she told them and hung up the telephone—only to pick it up again the next moment and order them to stop firing on the sick!

Tall, with her hair cut short, wearing a white dress or blouse and flat-heeled shoes, she has no time to waste on mirrors, which are nonexistent in her house! Lighting one cigarette from another, she walks from bed to bed, making her way between mattresses on the floor, stepping over bodies and children. On all sides, hands stretch out to her, patients smile at her. She stops and talks to them—she knows all the mountain dialects. Twelve thousand patients have passed through her hands since the days when she went from village to village trying to snatch children from death, children who were left to die without care because their parents were afraid to take them to the hospital. 'But it's been a long haul, and I often felt discouraged.'

She is American, and though her hospital is outside Kontum, she drives around in a car. She has no fear of the Vietcong. Perhaps because, in a certain way, the *montagnards* form a kind of bodyguard round her, and protect her.

When I left the hospital, it was the hour of prayer, and glancing back, I saw that all faces were turned towards . . . Dr. Smith's door! Although many have been converted by the missionaries, they still feel in their hearts that Ya Payang Ti (the grandmother of all medicine, as they call her) is part sorcerer, part miracle worker, and part white goddess.

The other memorable woman in Kontum is Sister Marie-Louise (whether she's Number One or Number Two, I don't know, and I don't want to start a 'war of women'). I must confess to a special fondness for her, though, and for the good Vietnamese sisters who surround her, for her lepers, for her personality, her spirits, her good humour and her rages. I meant to spend twenty-four hours at

Kontum, but already I had been at the leper colony for four days, fussed over and coddled. Surrounded by children, I suddenly realized that I'd had an overdose of war and anything that even faintly resembled a soldier. The sight of khaki made me sick.

'Ten years ago this was bushland,' Sister Marie-Louise told me.

Her village now has 300 adults and 200 children in it. The houses, the dispensary, the chapel, the school, the dormitories, the cinema—all have been built by lepers under the direction of Sister Marie-Louise who, as occasion demands, is architect, contractor, carpenter, or painter.

'The Americans help us a lot! The Special Forces, the Airborne, or the Air Force. Every time they receive fresh provisions, they bring us what's left of their canned goods—and that's important. At Christmas we were swamped with toys.'

She was about to make a distribution.

'You see, we don't give everything to our own children. I'll go into the forest and distribute some of these things to people who have nothing. You should have seen the children's faces when they saw Santa Claus coming down by parachute! Oh, yes, the G.I.s all came by air, their arms filled with presents! I still don't know who was happier. Perhaps those big boys felt less lonely surrounded by children, even if they were lepers, than they do in their camp. They all told me about their life, their children, and their wives back home in the United States. What a tragedy this war is! Come with me, we will go and ask Special Forces for a film. I speak badly, so you must explain to them that we want a decent film, not a questionable one like last time.'

I followed her. For that matter I had no choice—she dominated me, and I let her.

She strolls around the American camps as if she were at home and all the G.I.s know her.

'You must come to dinner with them one evening. They're so lonely.'

She was even making dates for me! Although I am Catholic, I had never in my life been so surrounded by nuns' veils, and I was full of enthusiasm for the life they were leading here.

'Oh, but there are sisters and sisters!' Marie-Louise told me, shaking her head.

The Benedictines of Ban Me Thuot, who are now in Kontum for

a few days, are about to give up what they've taken ten years to build. They want to get still closer to the mountain people, because they feel that they don't know them or understand enough about them.

When I met their Superior, Mother Colombo, she explained, 'We are going to study with Monsignor the best way to get closer to the Rhadé tribe, perhaps by going from village to village, and living in a very simple, monastic way.'

As for Mother Boniface, granddaughter of the Emperor of Austria, she used a marvellous expression. 'It's tremendous. To begin all over again! Not to end like an old maid!' I found them both admirable.

I spent my evenings listening to Sister Marie-Louise telling stories about the *montagnards*, their lives, their customs. It was too bad that I didn't have a tape recorder with me!

'If many of them are Communists, it is the fault of the Vietnamese, who have always despised them! The Vietcong know how to win them over.

'Among the Jarai, when a mother dies in childbirth, they bury the child, too, between her legs. All the Jarai are buried in the same grave, one immense tomb for each village and, every day, the women carry food to the dead.

'Every year, there is a festival of graves. Libations are poured. The leader invokes the spirit that creates life: everyone mates publicly— it doesn't matter with whom.

'The women are the first to drink rice alcohol from earthenware jars: this is a matriarchy.

'A first-born child buried at the foot of the stairs brings good luck to the new family.

'Children do as they please, when they please, and are never reprimanded.

'Boys go with a girl as soon as they are able to. Once engaged, it is serious. They are promised, and they wait.'

I could have listened to her all night long.

The next day we had a picnic with the children at 'Paradise', a retreat for missionaries. The sisters piled into the Land-Rover and off we set for Dakto. Popol came with us, too. He was my favourite little boy, and he followed me everywhere.

At Dakto there was tragedy: three Americans, a major, a captain, and a sergeant had been killed the night before in an ambush a mile and a quarter from the centre of the village.

'Then the planes came,' Father Dujon told me, 'the jets dived down less than a mile away from us. We could see both the pilots and the bombs. It lasted two hours.'

Father Dujon had spent six months as a prisoner of the Vietcong *montagnards*.

'They kept me tied up most of the time, often forgetting to give me anything to eat, as well. My propaganda for the good Lord did not please them.'

Beyond Dakto, are the Vietcong. Forest, still more forest, mountains—that's their kingdom. Fifteen months ago the population of Dakto was 1,050. There are now 8,000 refugees in the villages that have sprung up within two miles of the city. They surround and protect Dakto!

'But they themselves have no protection at all,' Father Arnoux pointed out.

There were no celebrations that evening in the American camp at Kontum: they were in mourning for their three comrades killed the night before, on the eve of the truce.

Before telling you how I spent the New Year, I'll describe my Christmas Day.

As I had foreseen, the Vietcong were at the rendezvous between Minh Hoa and Ban Me Thunt. That day I had breakfast with the Americans, tea with 'Victor Charlie',* and a dinner dance with the 'Frenchies'. Rather a full day, don't you think?

As you look at the map you may wonder why I didn't drive along the coast, continuing along Route 1 as far as Qui Nhon— apparently the most direct road.

However, there is no such thing as logic in Vietnam, and often the shortest road is not, in fact, the quickest or the least dangerous. On the coastal road to the north of Tuy Hoa, in spite of a brigade of the Fourth division—the South Korean White Horse division— the Vietcong hold a stretch of sixty-two miles of road, which they have completely blocked and gutted with explosives.

There was only one solution: the highlands, a long detour and the Vietcong road tax.

When convoys use that route about once a month to bring

* 'Victor Charlie'—V.C.—stands for Vietcong in radio messages.

supplies to Ban Me Thuot, an ambush is part of the run, in spite of air support and companies scattered along the road at points known as nerve centres.

On the last run—500 trucks—two captains were killed. On days when the road is open for the army, ordinary truck drivers who don't want to be caught between two fires stay quietly at home. There were not so many cars on the road as in the Delta. In more than a hundred miles I met perhaps twenty vehicles at the most.

The villages, built on piles and entirely surrounded by stockades made of stakes placed side by side, are few and far between. The peasants do not venture out on the road without a gun over their shoulder—and they do not venture very far, at that.

The grey and lowering sky helped to increase the loneliness that oppressed me as I covered mile after mile. I had to ford rivers, drive through mud and ruts, and keep going as best as I could by myself. With the water up to my knees, moving stones that blocked the river-crossings, and then a flooded engine, I had moments of discouragement!

When I saw the bonnet of a 404 raised and the driver working on it, I stopped to help him.

'Go on, Madame! Don't stop!' he said, looking frantic. 'Many Vietminh here!' I didn't need to be told twice.

Then for the first time there were well-made bends, and the road surface was in good condition. It was possible on such stretches to drive at full speed—that is, if your brakes were good! All the bridges had been blown up, and I always noticed the detours too late. Moreover, every three or four miles, the road had been ploughed up by mines and was a mass of mud and ruts.

Another car in trouble: all the passengers, terribly smart young men, tried to keep their balance on the dry patches, concentrating on nothing except keeping their beautiful suede shoes clean. After breaking two tow-ropes, the driver and I finally managed to drag the car free. But we were covered with mud from head to foot! The suede-shoes brigade were still spotless. As he drove off, the driver warned me, 'Don't drive fast, Madame. Many Vietcong. Stop immediately—otherwise they shoot.'

A little farther on, a truck driver passed me and put out his hand showing three fingers. Three kilometres away—it was too late to turn back! And besides, I didn't want to!

A double curve, an S-bend and six Vietcong—two at each bend of the curve. Black pyjamas, Ho Chi Minh sandals, guns—one of them a Chinese repeater—American belts and grenades. I took it all in, in the wink of an eye.

'Phap.'* I wanted to show my passport, but he made a sign that it was not necessary and glanced inside the car. 'A woman, a civilian, the truce, no weapons, she can go on,' they must have thought. A story without words.

However, I turned off the engine and got out of the car. I wanted to photograph them.

'No!'

I would have liked to start a conversation, but it was difficult. They spoke only Vietnamese.

'Cao Ky? Thieu Ky? Ho Chi Minh?'

With a burst of laughter they answered: 'Ho Chi Minh!'

One of them offered me his flask of tea. To thank him I offered him two packets of cigarettes, which he refused. I insisted. In the end he accepted them at an order from another man, who seemed to be in charge. A 404 truck arrived, and two of the men left me; one went to check the interior of the truck and the passengers, while the other collected the tax and made out the receipt. I took out some money—I would have liked to have had a receipt too, and I wanted to know whether they were going to tax me. But, smiling, they shook their heads. Then they opened the car door for me, and I was free to go on.

It had all gone as I'd thought it would. The Vietcong had been correct, had not made me pay the tax, and had let me pass. My heart wasn't beating faster, I had no fear at all. Their frank, open faces gave me confidence.

As the 404 passed me, the driver gave me a 'thumbs-up' and a broad, conspiratorial smile—now we were accomplices.

By the side of the road a magnificent N.L.F. flag hung on a bamboo stick. I remembered, perhaps none too soon, my visit to the Marines' booby-trap school, where a flag had been part of the set-up. I would go souvenir-hunting another time.

Ban Me Thuot had once been Bao Dai's hunting lodge. Now the M.A.C.V. has taken over the villa once used by the Emperor's guests. When the French were in power, ceremonies were arranged

* 'I'm French.'

for the Governor-General—the sacrifice of buffaloes, parades of elephants, and elaborate exchanges of vows. At that time France promised never to abandon the *montagnards*.

Covered with mud, I was offered for the first time in Vietnam not a shower, but a *bath*, a hot bath! It was really Christmas!

Later, with Colonel Jim Adamson, the senior officer, I found that we had mutual friends in Paris. He's the only American to have won the amateur golf cup at the Saint-Germain Club!

'Yes, I know,' he told me, 'the Vietcong collect taxes every day on the Ninh Hoa road—on the Pleiku road, too, but much less regularly. It would take a whole American division to stop them. Peace?' he went on, 'Not a job for the Americans but for the Vietnamese.'

And a little later:

'We're winning the war. The Vietcong here in this region are starving, and their morale is low.'

This was not the opinion of the planters!

'We have never been surrounded before—there have never been so many Vietcong in the neighbourhood as at this moment!'

All the French of the region had collected together to celebrate Christmas. An American journalist, bored with camp life, went with me. We were welcomed with open arms, and conversation flowed again.

'A year and a half ago the Vietcong came to me—ten of them. They told me "we want two million." I didn't have it. A week later, they ran into an ambush on their way to my place: two were killed. I got a letter: "We hope you had no hand in this affair. . . ." You explain to them, show them your accounts. They understand, even sympathise with you. You begin to breathe again. . . . But no; they still want two million. If you don't pay, they'll kidnap you. It is always the same old story!'

Another planter told us, 'Do you know that the plantation of the Benedictine Sisters has been attacked? Attacked by Government forces who even boasted of it! If I see a battalion of Vietcong crossing my plantation on their way to attack Ban Me Thuot, do you think I'm going to go and warn the M.A.C.V. or the authorities?'

The shocked 'No!' from my transatlantic colleague not only expressed his personal opinion. It was the reply that any American would have made.

'You don't understand at all! Paying the Vietcong in order to survive is one thing. But don't forget this: we have the same skin!'

And all, with one accord, changed the subject!

Before I left for Pleiku, I had lunch at the White House—'Chez two dark-skinned Matiniques' as Lartéguy calls them. 'Chez the Frenchies', as the Americans say.

I got some advice: 'Between Ban Me Thuot and Pleiku drive with your foot hard on the floor: you run the risk of a surprise attack not only by the Vietcong but also by the U.S. Air Force. They drop rockets the moment they see anything unusual!'

All the mountain villages on the edge of the road have put up stockades for protection.

At Bien Blech I lunched with the Special Forces. 'Do you know that yesterday the V.C. stopped a bus and killed a woman and her child? Only a mile and a half from here, where you saw the dead tree across the road. No, they don't behave as you think, with discipline and order. They strike and kill for no reason at all.'

'Perhaps they had reasons we don't know about. Perhaps it was the wife of a deserter, I don't know. . . .'

I was taken aside by the captain of the camp, who could not conceive that 'Victor Charlie' might be human.

'And what do you say when they send us the ears and noses of our Vietnamese they've killed or captured?'

I burst out laughing.

I answered, 'And what about it when certain Americans send their best girls in the States the ears and noses—or something else—they've cut off Vietcong corpses; when they send them by parcel post under the name of Smith to make it harder to trace the real culprit—what do you say that is? A joke?'

'No! It's war!'

We were both being insincere and obstinate.

The truth is that American troops have copied their Vietnamese soldiers, who take these trophies to help them keep count of the number of V.C.s they've killed. At least that is the excuse they give.

On 'the other side', American corpses are horribly mutilated when they fall into the hands of the Viets: they are found with their genitals in their mouths.

Moreover, atrocities lead to worse atrocities. American journalists are disturbed by these practices and have frequently warned the American high command.

I'll tell you about Pleiku, and about General Collins and General Vinh Loc another time. I have to pass through Pleiku again to get to An Khê.

And now at last, my New Year's Eve! At the leper colony!

By the light of a wood fire which they kept piling logs on, the lepers had come to wish Sister Marie-Louise a Happy New Year. Solos, choruses, dances—gay and wistful melodies. All the boys and girls in turn drew near the fire to do their number.

A disabled leper was carried in on a stretcher—he had no legs. Out of empty tin cans and some wire he had made an instrument from which he managed to draw sounds that were not too discordant.

'I found him on a forest track two months ago,' Sister Marie-Louise explained, 'in the middle of the road. I had only two choices: either to run over him or to take him with me.'

Then came the rhythmic tapping of the women on hollow bamboos, and finally the gongs. A young girl, very beautiful and shy, danced slowly, at the same time humming an infinitely sad tune. The firelight shone on her thick black hair and on her brown skin, and every eye was fixed on her, entranced.

The hand-woven border of her loincloth did not show the usual scenes of mountain life, but helicopters, aeroplanes and jeeps!

'She wove it herself,' Sister Marie-Louise mumured, 'and yet she never leaves the leper colony!'

The head of the community came to offer his greetings in hesitant French. Then, to round it off, a long procession led by gongs. . . .

I had passed from 1966 to 1967 in a very moving way.

11

In Search of a Vice-Consul

Saigon, January 10, 1967

Pat:

You may have seen a paragraph in the newspaper:
'French journalist discovers and sends to Saigon the body of Vice-Consul Jean Bion who was captured by the Vietcong and died in captivity about fifteen months ago.'

You have known me play many rôles already but you can never have imagined that one day you would hear of me setting off in search of missing bodies, as though it were a treasure hunt. All right; enough of jokes that border on the macabre and on bad taste.

I don't think I've already told you that in Kontum when I was studying the map of that region with Mgr. Seiltz and he was describing some of his wanderings to me (which have nothing on mine) he said, à propos of nothing in particular: 'Jean Bion is buried here, at Sung Le.'

'The Vice-Consul! But if they know where his grave is, why hasn't his body been shipped back to France? He died fifteen months ago.'

I was surprised, and shocked!

Since Camau, since the beginning of my 'crazy trip' (that term is getting on my nerves because so far my expectations have all proved to be correct) every time I stayed in a Frenchman's house, a planter or otherwise, the conversation always came back to this subject: 'What you are doing is dangerous. Remember Jean Bion, the French Vice-Consul. He was captured, and now he's dead.'

Also, the most unlikely rumours were circulating. At one moment he had been murdered by the C.I.A., the next he was still alive, a prisoner, somewhere or other, of the Communist *montagnards*. It was even said that the French Government had refused to pay a ransom for him so that they wouldn't have to give official recognition to the N.L.F.

But on one point everyone agreed: Jean Bion's kindness and

devotion had made him loved and appreciated everywhere. He was particularly concerned with the interests of French settlers outside Saigon. He often went to see them, and had established friendly relations with them.

Gradually, I began to develop a sort of posthumous friendship myself with this Vice-Consul, who was not afraid to drive on all the roads.

'Was he a prisoner a long time? How did he die? As the result of bad treatment?' I overwhelmed the bishop with questions.

'I'll begin at the beginning. He was captured in September 1965 as he was riding in a Vietnamese bus between Pleiku and Kontum. He planned to pay me a visit after stopping first at 'La Cateca,' the tea plantation at Pleiku.

'Despite the protests of the other passengers, who insisted that he was French and a Vice-Consul—he was the only white man in the bus—he finally had to pick up his little suitcase and follow the Vietcong—a few *montagnards* who had set up a block on the road to check vehicles and collect the taxes.'

'Did he die as the result of bad treatment? If so, I'll have to revise all my ideas about the N.L.F.'

'No, not at all. Besides, they were ready to free him when he fell ill. That was the time of *Pleimé*, of non-stop bombardments, a long and terribly difficult march—and the rainy season. To add to his bad luck, he was diabetic and could not take rice.'

I could not help smiling: to be captured by the Vietcong and not be able to eat rice is obviously a serious handicap to begin with.

'I know, from Catholics, from *montagnards* and through the grapevine,' Mgr. Seiltz continued, 'that they tried to do all they could for him. While waiting to verify his identity and his papers, they gave him chicken or fish whenever they could. When he was dying, they finally left him in a Catholic Vietnamese village—one of those Vietnamese villages set up by Diem* in the mountain country. Though he was nursed and watched over by the women, he died at Sung Le, two days later. I have statements from peasants who were there during his last moments and who later dug his grave.'

'But I still don't understand what followed. Why *is* his body still there?'

* The former head of South Vietnam was Catholic.

'A few days after his death, the village was bombed, then evacuated. At the time it was impossible to ask the Americans to risk men's lives to go looking for a corpse.'

'Fifteen months ago, that reasoning was valid,' I admitted. 'But surely not now. The Fourth Infantry Division, which landed about six months ago, has its command post at Pleiku. They are in charge of the whole area, which extends from Pleiku to the Cambodian frontier. I'm sure they must have passed through this village in the course of operations. Had they known, they could easily have got the body, and sent it home.' And on a sudden impulse I added:

'Couldn't we try together to see what can be done? Perhaps we could even go there by car! General Collins and Colonel Miller of the Fourth Division know me well, and they could tell us just what the position is.'

His response was evasive—in fact, a 'no'.

But Sister Marie-Louise said, 'As a journalist, acting on your own, you might pull it off. I would gladly go with you, but the visiting sister-in-charge doesn't like me to wander off so far by car when I have so much trouble on my hands with my lepers both here and in the neighbourhood.'

So I set out well pleased with myself, determined to do what I could to recover the body. Quite mad? Not from my point of view. Although I was indignant at the general indifference shown by the French over the recovery of the body, which was after all not just anybody's, I also felt that something of the kind might happen to me, in which case I should not be able to count on help from anyone. I didn't even have the advantage of belonging to the Diplomatic Service!

Sister Marie-Louise did not go with me, but she gave me Louis. 'He will always be of some use to you. He is a *montagnard* and speaks both French and Vietnamese. Put him on the bus to get him back to Pleiku. Don't worry, he is cured.' Because, of course, he was a leper!

But that was not all. . . . I also took a little boy of six, Popol, who had fallen for me as I had for him. He followed me everywhere and never left my side. An orphan, of leper parents, he was the darling of the good sisters.

'Just keep him for the rest of the trip. He will be company for you. He adores the car. When you get tired of each other, send him back by army plane. Don't worry, he knows how to behave. I take him to lunch at the Cabot Lodges* when I go to Saigon!'

Though Popol did not speak French, he understood it perfectly and we had no trouble understanding each other.

I took food for the journey and medicine, including, among other things, two boxes of a thousand tablets of Nivaquine.

'Give them to Pleimonou from me,' Sister Marie-Louise called to me. And then we were off.

We stopped at Pleiku for five minutes with Lieutenant Duchesne, press officer for the Second Corps.

'Right now, you can go on, Michèle. The road is mined every night, but a convoy and the mine clearance squads have just gone through.'

Built by the American army engineers, the road—a dirt track full of holes—leads to the Cambodian frontier and to the Second Brigade of the Fourth Infantry Division.

There were no Vietnamese on the road. No trucks, civilian cars or Lambrettas. Only two or three villages, and a few *montagnards* with hollow cheeks and feverish eyes: the result of years of under-nourishment. The road belonged to the convoys, which were driving hell for leather! At one bend in the road, I found myself bonnet to bonnet with a tank! Into the ditch—it was the only solution! Luckily, nothing broke.

At the Second Brigade, Popol promptly became the camp favourite, but he was so fascinated by the landings and take-offs that he had eyes only for the helicopters. About eight in the evening, while Jerry White was preparing a barbecue, and Colonel Judson Miller, Colonel Lay, Colonel Lonsburg, and Colonel Morley were all on their knees around Popol who, tongue between his teeth, was trying to write his name, Popo . . . suddenly, the first mortar shell landed a few yards from us!

All the lights went out, and there I was, flat on my stomach crawling and dragging the little boy by the hand—and muttering to myself, 'You're mad, Michèle, this is war. And here you are with Popol.'

My tight skirt prevented me from running, and all the foxholes were already occupied: the Second Brigade had changed position the day before, and there was a wild scramble to find shelter.

* United States Ambassador at that time.

Hн

At last, Colonel Lay called, 'This way, Michèle.' Popol, indifferent to everything that was happening around him, peacefully fell asleep at the bottom of our foxhole, with a bulletproof jacket for a blanket.

As always, in such situations, you count the bangs, you remember the other times. That makes you think, 'I got away with it before! Why not today?'

The noise of rockets, and of tracer bullets from the 'dragon ships' (old Dakotas armed with cannons) took over from the mortars. Forty minutes later, it was all over. There was no more to do but count the wounded—twelve—and the craters—about 150.

A long line of trucks, behind our tent, had been destroyed, but without them, the Colonels, Popol, and I would all have been wounded.

As for the Vice-Consul, I'd almost forgotten about him in the midst of this interlude. But when things had quietened down, Colonel Judson Miller put me in the picture.

'Sung Le,' he said, 'is on a link-road between two others which radiate out from Pleiku until they reach the frontier of Cambodia. Although convoys pass daily over the two roads there is little traffic on the link-road, so the problem of mines is serious.

'The village itself was abandoned fifteen months ago and is now quite overgrown. You may as well look for a needle in a haystack if you don't go with someone who knows the exact position of the grave. Your best bet is to try the refugees' village about two miles from 'La Cateca', the French tea plantation.

'If you consider it necessary, ask the One/Ten Cavalry of the First Division for a helicopter. It can't set down—that's a danger zone—but it will watch over you from a distance. Speak to Major Shaughnessy.'

And as a parting shot he added, 'Don't forget that last night's attack was almost in the line of your village, in any case not very far from it.' A reassuring thought!

The road was not exactly the N.7 and signposts were scarce. On leaving the camp I set off in the opposite direction to Pleiku heading straight for Cambodia!

We got bogged down in the forest and, still obsessed by last night's attack, Louis never stopped repeating:

'Many Vietcong, Madame! Not good here!'

We'd hardly finished freeing the car after superhuman efforts—

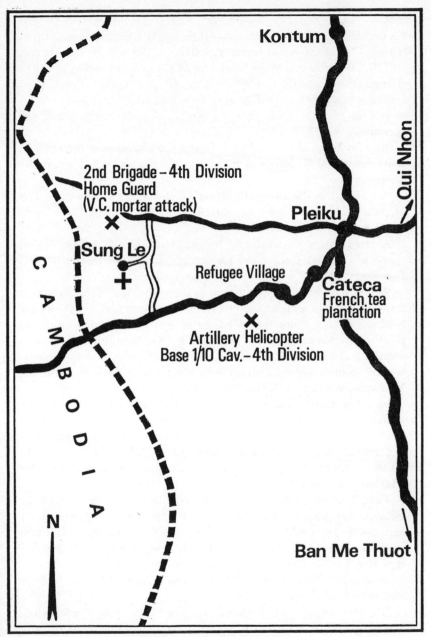

In search of a Vice-Consul.

his fear was becoming infectious—when two G.I.s came tearing up in a Jeep. One of them was James T. Baikcum, Colonel Miller's driver.

'Oh, you managed to get free! The M.P.s saw you go by, but they thought they were dreaming!'

'She's heading for the frontier,' they told us. 'There are no convoys today; what with the ruts and the mud, she'll never get through.'

'So you came after me. But I thought it was against the rules to drive around with less than three armed vehicles. What about the Vietcong?'

'Yes, but I'm the Colonel's driver, so the M.P.s let me pass. The Vietcong? I never gave them a thought.'

'Thanks, Jim. Thanks a lot.'

At last I reached 'La Cateca', the tea plantation. Two Frenchmen, 'pre-war colonials', at least as far as their clothes went, were the last Europeans to have seen the Vice-Consul alive.

'Mme. Bion has often written to us through one of their friends at the embassy. As well as the emotional strain on her, so long as her husband's body is not recovered, he is reported "missing" with all the legal inconveniences that that entails. We haven't had time to do anything about it. And then, too, our field of action is very limited: we are caught between the Vietnamese, the Americans, and the Vietcong. We can't risk one false step.'

In other words, for fear of trouble they refused to collaborate with me. Being stubborn by nature this only made me more determined. I sent Louis and Popol off in the bus to Kontum. The little boy was in tears and I was not dry-eyed myself, but I had already let them run too many risks. Now I was sending them back to Sister Marie-Louise, to safety.

Then I set off in search of the refugee village and the head of the village, the Vietnamese priest who fortunately spoke French. I explained my problem and found myself confronted with two peasants who—with the priest acting as interpreter—told me either that they had dug the grave, or had seen Monsieur dying.

'Good. You'll be rewarded later. Come with me in the Dauphine and we'll find the place today.'

'They're afraid. They don't want to,' the priest translated, laughing. But he laughed on the other side of his face an hour later when they insisted that he should come with us!

However, the company of the good Lord was not enough for them—they still hesitated. Inspiration! I explained to them that a helicopter would fly just over our heads. Very well, they would go. Now I just had to find Major Thomas Shaughnessy.

Among the rows of tents of the First Cavalry and the Fourth Infantry Division, all jumbled up together, it took me an hour to run to earth the one with the flight schedules for helicopters of the 1/10 Cavalry of the Fourth Division.

'I will give you not one but two helicopters; that's the rule,' Major Shaughnessy told me, happy to be able to lend me a hand.

A G.I. stopped me on the way out. 'You can't imagine how restful to the eyes your white car seems. Don't say you're a journalist! I'd rather think of you as a tourist: in a way, I feel as if I'm one, too. I've been here six months and I haven't met "Victor Charlie" yet. I drive a big green truck, that's all!'

I shall pass over the breakdown about a mile south of the fork in the road, and the helicopters which had to go back, but which I recalled by tank radio. On the bumpy track the slightest thing roused my suspicions . . . a hole, even a fallen branch . . was a sign.

Also I had to stop every five minutes, for my three heroes were frightened to death and had to be comforted! At last we turned left on to a still worse track, and then after a mile or so, the church . . the only building still standing, although its roof had been blown off.

'Now we'll have to walk for 500 yards or so!'

It was my turn to have cold shivers! A walk was not included in in my programme. But I couldn't turn back now.

Though the helicopters reassured my companions, they worried me. All they could do was draw attention to us. But they were a *sine qua non* for my guides, and I had to accept them.

We had no trouble spotting the great cross in the cemetery, but it took us more than half an hour to find Jean Bion's grave, hacking our way through the jungle with a machete. Even then I wasn't sure it was really his grave.

In case it wouldn't be possible to return next day with a truck, I took off the shirt I was wearing under my sweater and tied it on a stick to mark the exact position, and later take a photograph of it from a helicopter.

Back at the plantation I announced, 'I've found the exact spot of the grave. If you like, we can go there tomorrow in the Land-Rover!'

They wouldn't go with me. 'With the plantation on our hands we can't take any chances of having an accident,' they said, but they lent me the car.

'Too bad if it's blown up by a mine.' They'd give me a coffin, though—'the other one will have rotted'—and some shovels and picks. I picked up my guides again—though the priest could not be found. And still hanging on to the steering wheel for dear life, we drove back to the site of the grave with the helicopters flying above us. My shirt was no longer tied the way I'd left it. As I walked along, I started to change the roll of film in my camera, and I had my head lowered when suddenly I saw a great hole packed with sharpened sticks—a 'Viet' trap! A bamboo stake went right into my foot. I couldn't stop the blood flowing, but I was the only one who could drive. . . .

With the helicopters circling above us, and making an infernal racket, my 'friends' began to dig. Sure enough, just as they'd said the evening before, there really was a body there, about three feet below the ground, feet pointing towards the cross. The coffin that once contained it had completely rotted away. Then began a macabre operation.

The return trip was more than painful. My foot hurt badly, and my nerves were beginning to give way. We had to be careful not to jolt the corpse. My Vietnamese who were playing the part of mourners were no help at all. I was half-way between an attack of hysterics and floods of tears.

I paid them for their services, dropped them off in their village, and then went straight to the medical officer of Pleiku, to whom I explained my adventures and the nature of my load.

'We'll have it sent to Saigon for you.'

I was exhausted, so I left it all in the hands of Sergeant Rose and Lieutenant Duchesne, who very kindly and sympathetically took charge of everything. At the airfield a freight plane about to take off agreed to take my load, which had been placed in an ordinary packing box addressed to François Pelon, Agence France-Presse, Saigon. I was not at all sure that the Vietnamese had not dug up one of their own people—in which case I would certainly be in trouble with the authorities.

The telephone lines were out of order—you know what the telephone's like here!

'Don't worry,' the press officer told me. 'We'll call Tan Son Nhut by radio. They will notify François Pelon.'

And the next day, feeling much better, I set out—by plane—for Danag, where I intended to spend the weekend relaxing on the beach, after a week of living on my nerves.

That Saturday, about six in the evening, I finally managed to get Saigon on the phone. No one had notified the A.F.P. After three hours in the baggage room, the coffin had finally been taken to the American mortuary. As for François Pelon, he had received a telephone call: 'Michêle Ray is in a box.'

While he was trying to get through by telephone to France to tell my family—and prevent the agencies from cabling the news—he went to the mortuary at Tan Son Nhut.

'No,' an American guard told him. 'You are French. Come back with an official.' He then went back to Saigon and returned with Colonel Fraddy, the head of press services. There, of course, they were in for a surprise. It wasn't me 'in the box!' You can imagine his fury and his relief!

As for the Consul—not Bion, of course, but Lambroschini, the Consul General—he said to me very coldly, 'I congratulate you on your initiative and courage.'

So once again I am writing to you from Saigon, for I had to come here to sign a statement concerning my 'discovery' of the Vice-Consul. A discovery that was not really one at all, for the consulate had a plan in its archives showing the exact position of the grave!

Before I leave, I am going to take time to write to the only people who helped me, and thank them—the Fourth Infantry Division and the Air Force.

12

The Diehards of Pleiku

Qui Nhon, January 13, 1967
Dear old Pat,

At Pleiku, after handing over awards to the 'first of the twelve' of the Second Brigade, commanded by Colonel Lay, General Collins, Commander of the Fourth Division Infantry, asked me to describe and show him on a map my trip from Ca Mau.

'Do you know,' he said, 'that from Pleiku you can go as far as the Cambodian frontier? We have convoys every day. It was impossible a year or even eight months ago.'

'I know. A year ago I wouldn't have got as far as this without difficulties. To start with there was the Delta, where kidnappings and random hold-ups on the road were frequent. Over towards Tay Ninh there was the toll. The road between Ban Me Thuot and Pleiku had its own toll, too, like the Pleiku–Kontum road (it was on that run that the Vice-Consul was captured). As for venturing on the road to Dakto, that was running straight into the arms of the Vietcong.'

'Everyone has his own idea of peace in a country at war, Michèle,' said General Collins,' 'Ambassador Cabot Lodge's idea is this: "When every Vietnamese can move about freely without fear of being blown up by a mine, or being kidnapped or shot, then I think we will have made real progress." We're not there yet, but perhaps we're moving in that direction with very slow steps!

'Certainly the Vietcong have lost ground, and some key areas; they appear to have been driven back into the mountains: but they're still there, all around us.'

And as if to justify his statement, the military base at Pleiku has been attacked by mortar fire this week, three nights running. Three nights in the shelters! My companions in misfortune have been different each time, but the little story that's going the rounds in Vietnam at the moment, is always the same:

'Have you heard the one about the poor boy, the poor Vietcong who comes down from Hanoi over the Ho Chi Minh Trail carrying a mortar shell in each arm. Four months marching over the mountains, through the jungle, with malaria, incessant bombing from planes, and always hunger. Exhausted, he finally arrives at the gun site. One! Two! *bang! bang!* In twenty seconds it's all over.

'The officer in charge turns to him.

'"Go and get two more . . . from Hanoi!"

'The poor little Vietcong runs and runs as fast as he can. He runs to the other side, to defect!'

At this point everyone is supposed to laugh.

How many 'poor little Vietcong' were there on the three nights I told you about? Surely a whole battalion. I saw some of those soldiers in the Vietnamese prison in Pleiku. Most of them had been captured during Operation Irving, near Phu Cat—a joint effort by the American First Cavalry and the South Korean Tiger Division.

'Here, they've collected the diehards together,' I was told by General Vinh Loc's aide who accompanied me to the prison. 'Their stories are all alike; they come from Hanoi which they left more than a year or even fifteen months ago by the Ho Chi Minh Trail.'

But it was difficult to get more information, for voices were quickly raised in anger between the interpreter and the prisoner, or between the prisoner and the aide. I don't understand a word of Vietnamese, but from their attitudes, from their eyes, I sensed that all was not roses!

'Impossible to question them,' said the interpreter. 'They reduce everything to a political issue, to their faith in victory, and they spit on Ky and Thieu, calling them puppets who have sold out to the imperialists.'

But slowly and patiently I got him to prolong the interview.

One young boy—he was seventeen, though I would have said thirteen—had left Hanoi thirteen months ago:

'My job was moving rice—from one headquarters to another—in the jungle. That was all our group did. Very few of us were armed.'

Another boy, aged nineteen, was captured in an underground hospital which the Americans discovered.

'I had an attack of malaria.'

'Didn't you take pills regularly?'

'No. They were kept for serious cases—if they were lucky!'

After cross-checking with other statements, it seemed to me that this problem of malaria—and of medicines—is one of the chief difficulties of the Vietcong during their long marches and their life in the forest.

'Were you badly treated when you were questioned after your capture?'

Again their eyes blazed, and out came a flood of violent language which the interpreter refused to translate.

Two months before, when I had attended an interrogation of prisoners by the Fourth Division, the day after an operation, some of the prisoners had begged the Americans to keep them, not to turn them over to the Vietnamese. But whether they were captured by the Americans, the South Koreans, the Australians, or the Vietnamese, they all had to be questioned by the Vietnamese Government Information Service.

There was one question I had been dying to ask from the start. I told them the story of my journey. 'What would happen if I were captured?'

'You would be killed by the roadside, and your mutilated body would serve as an example.'

'You would first be tried and then condemned.'

Though the replies varied, the final message was always the same. They raised their voices, they became heated and upset.

'Don't you know that a journalist is only an observer?' I said. 'Don't you know that de Gaulle is against American policy in Vietnam?'

'De Gaulle? Never heard of him. With all these lackeys around you, you can only be a dirty imperialist. No torture would be good enough. Your ears and your nose would be cut off. But to begin with . . .'

The interpreter refused to translate this last remark. I imagine that my femininity would be in danger!

The aide brought the visit to an end, saying again:

'In spite of three months in camp, they are still rebels!'

'Here is one who speaks French, Major,' the interpreter said.

He looked harmless enough, but what he really thought he would not say—there were too many people about.

All I could learn was that he belonged to an army theatrical troupe which had been captured at Phu Cat—a dozen actors, among them two women. All of them came from Hanoi. He himself was a native of Annam, from Hué. In giving me his name he made it clear: 'I have four brothers fighting on the Government side.'

With special permission from the head of the camp, he gave me one of his paintings on wood: women in a rice field.

At the Vietnamese officers' club, I dined with General Vinh Loc, three officers, and their wives. General Vinh Loc commanded the Vietnamese troops of the Second Army Corps, in the area of the highlands. After graduating from the military college of Saumur in France, he rose to be a major in the French army. He is also one of the few Vietnamese who are taller than I am!

Having caught me examining the décor of the club—mosaics, velvets, soft lights, concealed mirrors—he told me, 'No, this is not luxury, it is a necessity. Relaxation for the warrior! It didn't cost me anything, for it was all done with part of the money belonging to the Diem family. American officers are always welcome!'

But only a few days before, the Americans had told me, 'We get rooked every time we put our foot in the place. And they even wanted to have a mixed club so they could come and help themselves at the P.X. We refused!'

'Your journey is most interesting,' Vinh Loc continued. 'But are you sure it was the Vietcong you saw on the road from Ban Me Thuot and not our *poor* Home Guard Forces?'

'With Ho Chi Minh sandals and Chinese repeating rifles?' I burst out laughing. 'No! I don't think so!'

'Do you know there is a very pretty love story behind the kidnapping of an American soldier by the Vietcong,' Vinh Loc told me. 'After two months in Saigon, an Air Force sergeant had been transferred here to Pleiku. But he had left his heart behind with a Vietnamese girl in Saigon. Not being able to fly down to see her for the weekend without official permission, he "borrowed" a jeep and some road maps and drove like a madman down the road to Saigon. They found his jeep just beyond Ban Me Thuot. But his love story apparently did not melt the Vietcongs' heart, for he is still a prisoner.'

To close a long discussion on America reactions to the war in Vietnam, he said: 'American opinion is like a bouillabaisse!'

I have been so taken up by my Vice-Consul that I have told you very little, I think, about 'La Cateca', the largest tea plantation in Vietnam: 2,200 acres.

One of their problems is to transport their harvest which must be sent to Saigon, since merchant shipping does not call at Qui Nhon. Like the oil companies, they make use of Vietnamese truckers, who in turn have to contend with road blocks and tolls.

To fill in their weekends on the plantation, in the midst of the Home Guard, of the A.R.V.N. and the Vietcong, 'my friends' the two planters, have set up observation posts and they hunt. Hunt who or what, you ask? Tigers, of course. Hasn't the head of state, Thieu, set the example? Almost every weekend he hunts baby tigers near Phan Rang. In the midst of B-52 raids, bombs, napalm, and Vietcong mortars, Thieu hunts tigers in Vietnam! What a a splendid headline for *France-Soir*!

Do you want any more little stories, more gossip? . . . There's one about the young girls from Pleiku who snubbed the Government soldiers because they didn't have enough money. To get revenge, the 'Red Berets' rounded up a few of the girls and raped them before letting them go back to Pleiku—naked.

You may have heard, perhaps, of that girl—Mamie Stover—who 'worked' the warships during the Pacific campaign. Pleiku has its Mamie Stover, too! It's not the ships this time, that serve as 'boudoirs', but all the tanks lined up along the roads round Pleiku. A home from home for the fighting man!

During dinner with the planters I was told: 'You are lucky that the Home Guard and the Government forces left us a few chickens and some lettuces.' (There is pilfering every day, they tell me.)

'You don't protest?'

'No. Except yesterday when I knew they had filched some chickens in a mountain village belonging to the plantation. Then I went to see the head of the province.'

'If I understood correctly, you have not only Government troops, but also Vietcong on the plantation. Aren't there often clashes between them?'

'Very rarely! They take great care to avoid each other. If you look at the bullet marks in the trees or on the walls of the buildings, not one of them is less than six feet high!'

As I left Pleiku on the An Khê road—that calls up memories for

you, doesn't it?—there was a police check. It is forbidden to transport weapons, and also rice, except under armed escort.

'For the Vietcong,' Vinh Loc had told me, 'rice is as important
as ammunition!'

Before leaving An Khê I went to see the only Frenchman there,
a missionary. 'When the Americans came,' he said, 'the Vietcong
had already surrounded the village and were about to take it.'

The same view was expressed by the Franciscan Sister of the leper
colony at Tuy Hoa, two miles from Qui Nhon. 'If you represent one
of those newspapers that are fiercely anti-American on principle,
just say so at once. We will give you something to eat and you can
get on your way. I am anti-Communist, and I don't hesitate to say
so. Ask the Mother Superior, who lived in China, then in North
Vietnam before all the missions were evacuated to the South in
accordance with the Geneva convention. Ask her! If the Americans
had not come eighteen months ago, Qui Nhon and the leper colony
would be occupied. We would no longer be here! As for my
patients. . . .'

I burst out laughing. I was impossible to stop her flood of words.
Besides, taking no notice at all of replies, she was calmly going about
setting the table.

A beach four miles long with coconut palms—that is the domain
of the Franciscan Sisters who have built their leper village on the
seashore—there are about 600 of them. Hospital buildings, chapel,
reception villa, school, and communal dwellings as well as private
villas . . . all the interiors are tiled: walls, ceilings, floors. It's gay, it
shines, it's clean!

'Our lepers make the tiles, and we have an oven to bake them,'
the Sister told me and smiled at my astonished expression.

I must confess that I have never seen in Europe, or in any
other place, for that matter, such a spotlessly clean hospital as
theirs.

By explaining that the lepers had done all the work, the
Sister forestalled the inevitable remark: 'That must have cost a
fortune!'

'The guest dining-room, as you must have noticed, is very large.
The Americans often come to see us. They are so glad to have lunch
here. It is a change from their camp!'

But at Qui Nhon the Americans are not fighting—that's the South

Koreans' job. The only Americans are engineers at the supply base. Instead of a battlefield, there's a magnificent beach and . . . eighty American nurses. What more could you ask for?

A rustic wooden chapel! After the marriage service, two couples emerge, the bridegrooms wearing carnations in their button-holes, the women in fragile long white dresses. Beneath the porch the souvenir photo is taken. The lawn and the benches are thronged with people; handfuls of rice are thrown in all directions and mingling with the cries of joy and congratulation, the sound of the harmonium can be heard once more. Bridesmaids in elaborate blue dresses and little hats . . . two Chevrolets, with white ribbons and flowers. And the inevitable sign: 'Just married'.

No, Pat, I am not somewhere in a little provincial town, but still in Qui Nhon.

By moving away a little, say about 200 yards, you would notice that the chapel is the camp chapel and that hundreds of children, their eyes opened wide in surprise, are pressed against the bars of the camp gates. 'Happy honeymoon!' 'The best of luck!' I, too, had tears in my eyes as I watched Cathy Ward, a sparkling brunette, and Mary Bates, a pretty, serious-looking blonde, on the arms of their brand-new husbands. Love story in Vietnam: two American nurses have just got married; one, to a male nurse, the other, to a doctor—both Americans too. As for David Vollmer, best man for one of the husbands, and his wife Joan, both of them nurses, they live in a 'charming little house', with a patio, in the centre of the camp. They have been in Qui Nhon six months.

More than ever, the unexpected is playing a part in my journey. At the headquarters of the South Korean Tiger Division, ten miles from Qui Nhon, I spent the morning watching the compulsory daily training in *takuendo* (Korean karate). Afterwards I lunched with the commanding officer, General Lew Bionh Hyun and his staff.

You remember the Korean in *Goldfinger*? That is more or less it. With the side of the hand they can, at will, break fifteen bricks, not to mention a man's spine. In the field, on active service the training goes on. And there, no doubt to keep their hand in when they're going into action against the Vietcong, the M.16 is often discarded in favour of their own 'arms'. Since their arrival in Vietnam—they now number 45,000—the South Koreans have built up a sound reputation as 'real soldiers', to which is often added the epithet 'killers'. The American professionals, those who fought in Korea, are proud of them.

'That's why we're in Vietnam as well. Fifteen years ago they were like the majority of the South Vietnamese, they either didn't know how to fight or they didn't want to. Look at them today.' Real mercenaries!

A museum of weapons salvaged after Operation Irving (Sept. 23–Oct. 28, 1966): two wax figures wearing the North Vietnamese uniform mount guard over this display which ranges from M.16s to American radios, from the latest model loudspeakers to sewing machines . . not to mention gas masks, and American, Chinese, and French medical supplies. There is also a tally of casualties: KIA (killed in action) 1,105; VCC (Vietcong captured) 467; WP (weapons) 449; HG (hand grenades) 866; etc.

The South Koreans cover an area that has increased from 14,000 square kilometres to 20,000 after Operation Meng Ho 6.

Captain Kim, the press officer, overwhelmed me with figures: 20,000 square kilometres for a population of 45,000 inhabitants. 'We need 7 men per square kilometre to protect 32 civilians. There has never been any sign of an attack on the pipeline that links Qui Nhon to An Khê, in spite of the fact that it is vital to the First Cavalry Division. We guarantee their security as well as the road and the pass. A jeep can move about there alone, and our men can go unarmed.'

The art of *takuendo* is perhaps enough to drive off the most determined Vietcong.

One thing struck me on the way to the camp; in the villages the children do not run after the South Korean soldiers as they do after the G.I.s. There is some sort of barrier between them. Is it fear, or respect? Perhaps both. Perhaps, too, their parents remember that it was the Koreans who guarded the camps at the time of the Japanese occupation.

Three American divisions, two Korean divisions, three Vietnamese divisions . . that makes up the Second Army Corps, in the area of the highlands. There are zones of peace—that is, apparent peace, and zones where war rages. At Bong Son, I am going into one of the latter zones, and I'm really scared.

This will be war in earnest, war where there's no longer room for surprises.

I'm very depressed. I must be tired, too. Unless perhaps, I'm brooding about the treatment the prisoners promised me in the camp at Pleiku if I'm captured.

No matter how often I tell myself that they were 'diehards', as General Vinh Loc's aide-de-camp called them, nor how much I try to think that after three months of camp, three months of prison, it is only natural that their minds would be filled with thoughts of murder, nevertheless I find it hard to sleep. . . .

At Pleiku, General Collins (in the centre, with glasses) commanding the Fourth Infantry Division, tells me 'Everyone has his own idea of peace in a country at war. Cabot Lodge's is: 'When even Vietnamese can move about freely without fear of being blown up by a mine, or being kidnapped or shot, then I think we will have made real progress.'

The 1/12 of the Second Brigade of the Fourth Infantry Division is decorated.

By mistake, I turned right towards the Cambodian frontier. Jim, Colonel Miller's driver, came to look for me in spite of the rule against travelling without an armed escort. 'And the Vietcongs?' 'I'm not a professional,' he told me, 'I never gave them a thought.'

Men of the L.L.D.B., the Vietnamese Home Guard.

In a mountain village, with the Benedictine Sisters of Ban Me Thuot (in the foreground), and (right at the back) one of the 'tigresses', Sister Marie-Louise.

Popol, the little mountain boy who lives in Sister Marie-Louise's leper hospital at Kontum. He went everywhere with me. Luckily I'd sent him back to Sister Marie-Louise before my capture.

A woman and her little boy on a bicycle. There are thousands of bicycles, everywhere.

Tuesday, January 17, 11.30 a.m. Two kilometres past Bong Son-English, I am stopped by armoured cars. This is the border of the zone controlled by the Vietcong—these women and children are Vietcongs.

Tuesday, January 17, midday. Three kilometres further on, a puncture. Two Vietnamese students help me repair it (here you see one of them with a hat). I swung the car round, but I hadn't gone 500 yards when three Vietcongs appeared.

The Bong Son road where I was captured.
(*Simon Pietri; Holmes Lebel*)

The M.A.C.V. issued an order that no one was to look for me. These are my journalist friends who, with Government soldiers, discovered my car, camouflaged and rigged with booby traps. (*Simon Pietri; Holmes Lebel*)

PART III

Captive of the V.C.

13

The Road is Cut

'I'm going to fly over the Bong Son road and beyond. Come with me,' suggested Colonel Bush, who was in command of the 45th engineering battalion, the army engineers of the second tactical zone. 'You can see for yourself exactly what the position is and find out whether you have a chance of getting through in the Renault.'

In a one-engine plane, with pilot and co-pilot, we flew at a low altitude. 'This section, between Qui Nhon and Bong Son, was opened for military use four months ago,' the Colonel said, 'following a combined operation involving the South Koreans and the First Cavalry—Operation Irving. Afterwards, torrential rain carried away bridges and embankments in the rice fields. My men have just finished putting them right: they were re-opened yesterday. The work was made very difficult by daily ambushes and sniping.'

To the north of Bong Son, military convoys, Vietnamese trucks, and Lambrettas have disappeared from the road. The only sign of movement is a few Vietnamese in black pyjama-suits and cone-shaped hats. On foot or on bikes, they avoid the difficult points by cutting through the rice paddy.

But I must keep to the point. There are about fifty miles that are virtually impossible to cover by car, jeep, or any other vehicle: barricades of branches that are certainly mined, sections of road completely torn up.

'It is occupied territory, controlled by the Vietcong just as it was four months ago south of Bong Son,' said Bush. 'The "Viets" have set up a system of ferries with a toll station at every blown-up bridge.'

The landscape—the rice paddy—looks like a sieve, full of craters left by artillery fire or bombs. Even the side of the mountain is scorched by napalm. I have been in Vietnam six months, but I

have rarely seen a more desolate countryside and I was distressed
by it. The enemy opened fire on us. We gained altitude and turned
back to Qui Nhon with a bullet in our tail.

'What do you plan to do?' the colonel asked me as we landed.

'Go straight to Bong Son, put the car on a military or a civilian
boat as far as Quang Ngai, then go on to the 17th Parallel. I would
like to come back here during the Têt and take advantage of the
truce to cross that crater zone, the 'sieve'. On foot or on a bike?
I don't know. But I really would like to see what is going on down
there.',

Binh Dinh has always been the black spot of my travels. There are
many snipers, daily ambushes, and any minute a mine can go off.
The feverish activity of Qui Nhon, the mud in the streets, which
you take with you everywhere, the invitations it's hard to refuse,
the nurses who rush back and forth and talk too loudly . . . I suddenly
needed quiet; I needed to feel at home again and I like Saigon on
Sundays. . . . So I flew back to the capital.

No military convoys, but civilian cars moving freely about, and
relaxed Vietnamese strolling hand in hand. Kennedy Square at the
top of Tu Do street, where the cathedral stands, looked like the
main square in any provincial town when people are coming out of
church. For a change, it was not very hot and the bangs of the jets
scarcely rattled the windows.

I shall think of this day often in the future—my last weekend of
peace before returning to the war! For a whole week I had been
under fire from Vietcong mortars. And I still didn't know that Sunday that I'd soon be under fire from American guns, living through
the hell of an aerial bombardment.

Monday, January 16
Got up at three o'clock. Tan Son Nhut, the C.130 . . . Qui Nhon at
nine o'clock. The car on the airfield, my things already on board.
Army boots are not high enough for this mud. I tried in town to
find some other rubber ones. I don't know who they're made for,
but the sizes begin here at 45 or 46, so I gave up the search. From
my knees down I was still a soldier—and I lived to regret it!

Qui Nhon Phu Cat
This sector is patrolled by South Koreans. Signs and notices are

either in Vietnamese, English, and Korean, or simply in Vietnamese and Korean. The children shout 'O.K. give me five pis' in Korean. Trucks pass through every morning on their way to fetch a load of refugees (there are about 40,000 of them altogether) from one of the numerous camps in the area. Taken to their fields, which have been neglected during the fighting, the peasants cultivate the rice, guarded by armed soldiers. In the evening, the same journey in reverse; the trucks bring them back. Those nearer their fields line the roads on foot, trotting quickly along with their balancing-poles on their shoulders.

I stopped at one of the camps. The trees have all been levelled by bulldozer and the area surrounded by wire netting to protect them, apparently from Vietcong reprisals. An extra alarm-system: empty beer or Coca Cola cans hang on the barbed wire! In huts with corrugated-iron roofs whole families are crowded together with all their possessions—often just a small bundle of things they were able to save, when they were evacuated from their houses—often by force—during the bombing. A cooking pot perhaps, and a few bowls in the luckier cases.

Representatives from American Civil Aid do the best they can. But they are snowed under by the endless flow of new refugees. There are a few successful schemes which are exceptions to the rule: for instance, distribution of milk for children. A large vat, a ladle and a paper cup for each child standing in a long queue. Distributed in any other way, the milk would never reach their mouths, but would be intercepted on its journey by certain 'responsible' Vietnamese or by the families themselves. Somehow or other, the cartons would reappear on the stalls of the small dealers who line the roadside near the camp.

A class for children is being organized under canvas. They have set it up as an emergency measure, but it's an emergency that's in danger of lasting a long time.

I was tugged and jostled from all sides, my clothes were almost torn off me. Hands reached out, children, and women with babies at their breasts . . . or crying. Their eyes have seen too many horrors. They are completely destitute. There is nothing left for them. Only the old women look indifferent and vague, their lips and teeth stained dark red from chewing betel-nut. They have known worse things in their time.

I had to get away from them, I almost ran. I could do nothing for them, and their suffering sickened me.

I met a company of South Koreans. Marching in perfect formation on either side of the road, they were a striking contrast to an A.R.V.N. company coming towards me—some distance away. They were all over the place, rifles swinging loosely in their hands, feet dragging, one man holding a chicken by its feet, another precariously clutching a bag full of eggs, another with a saucepan hanging on his belt. Little windfalls they'd collected from the population they're supposed to pacify—a great success, as you can imagine! Yet, when I photograph or film them, they can't resist posing like conquering heroes!

A jeep that had been following me since Phu My caught up with me and stopped.

'What are you doing here? I thought I must be dreaming.'

I must admit that I've learnt the knack of explaining myself and my journey in a few seconds. It was the senior medical officer of the First Cavalry Division and his assistant, who were on their way to Hammond.

'Come and have lunch with us.'

'Thanks a lot.' Of course I accepted.

(Sorry, Doc, but your name's been lost in the mists of memory. It was part of the list I forced myself to swallow the very next day—only a few hours after I left you.)

Without my guide I would have been lost; I would have gone round in circles. I would never have found the press centre or the headquarters of the 'airborne cavalry'.

On all sides great dumps of stores, a network of roads, notices I couldn't read, dozens of parking places that had just been tarred, helicopters that landed on newly-cleared ground almost before the dust had settled, and petrol tanks made of rubber which hadn't been used yet, waited in rows, stretched almost to bursting. Although I'm so used to American camps, they always take me by surprise. In queues fifty yards long, their trays in their hands, the G.I.s move forward between lengths of rope stretched from one little notice-board to another.

'As often as we can, we serve a hot meal a day to companies in the field,' the doctor told me. 'We try to vary the menu as much as possible.'

'How is it that men like these, with all their marching, and exercise, are still fat, flabby, and often pimply? I've gained ten pounds myself while I've been following the troops. Yet I've never been so active in my life.

'Our C.K. rations and others, have not been studied in relation to the climate. The whole thing ought to be revised. We're learning as we go along. But our number one problem is malaria. Especially at this moment—in the rainy season. The percentage of cases has never been so high.'

Officers don't have to wait outside, but under canvas. The conversation is lively.

'You must have a permit. It's impossible otherwise.'

'No,' I have to laugh, for everywhere they ask the same question and they're always sure they're right.

'Here it's perhaps a little different from the rest of Vietnam. This was one of the centres of Vietminh resistance during *your* war, and today it's one of the Vietcong centres: their defence is even better organized here than anywhere else. They hold a stretch of nearly forty miles north of Bong Son all to themselves. The road is cut. Here, Michèle, it's war, war to the death. Two North Vietnamese divisions and a V.C. regiment are in the valley of An Lao, their stronghold. Our convoys to Bong Son are attacked every time, and jeeps are blown up every day by mines.'

This was the reason why, a few minutes later, I decided not to wait for the next morning's convoy. I thought I would have less chance of falling into an ambush with a civilian car and with no military escort.

Colonel Wolf, the senior staff officer, a pleasant, understanding man, with a little moustache and a nylon scarf always tucked in the opening of his shirt, said to me in perfect French as I was leaving, 'So that you won't have to come back to Qui Nhon, a Caribou will stop by tomorrow afternoon at two o'clock to take you and your Renault to Bong Son-English. From there you can continue your journey to the 17th Parallel. Good luck!'

'Thank you, Colonel, that will save me a round trip on one of the most dangerous roads in Vietnam.'

After Hammond, only a few Lambrettas had ventured out. The 'gentleman's agreement' no longer applies. This is war! What with convoys, mines, and rainstorms—it is neither a road nor even a trail, but a regular quagmire. Nor is there any longer the friendly, generous help of the peasants of the Delta. These people are different —refugees, homeless and destitute, yet surrounded by Americans, and tempted by their affluence. I'm cheated every time—500 piastres, payable in advance, to push the car, even for a couple of yards! An American division near by makes every mile expensive!

Impossible to open the doors; the ruts were too deep. I was stuck and blocking the way for two Vietnamese military trucks that had been following me for a mile and a half. The driver of the first truck got out, sized up the amount of space left for him, tried to pass, and got stuck in his turn. Now there was only one thing for them to do: notice my presence at last. Looking tired already, the men jumped down on to the road, turned up their trouser-legs above their boots, picked their way gingerly through the mud to demand money for pushing me. For the locals, O.K.—for soldiers, no! They insisted. But I continued to act dumb. Hanging about on the road in a danger zone apparently did not appeal to them, either, so rolling up their sleeves and using only the tips of their fingers—they pushed. Their arrogance and their insolence infuriated me.

The road bridge before Bong Son had been blown up. It was the Americans, not the Vietnamese, who had placed a twenty-four-hour guard on the second bridge that carried the railway. A halt while the car was examined, inside, underneath, with a 'counter' to detect any mines, and an inspection of papers. One-way traffic, with a guard every few yards. Ten in all. The camp of the 22nd Vietnamese Regiment and a battalion from the First Cavalry Division was stationed a mile or two to the north, not at Bong Son, but at Te Duc, nicknamed 'English'.

A church destroyed by bombing, then a sign: *English*. The most advanced camp in Binh Dinh, except for the Vietnamese company at Tam Quan, already has a landing strip capable of taking C.123s. Although I was covered with mud from head to foot, I was welcomed with open arms.

'But you can't go any farther,' Major Porter and Colonel Nguyen of the 42nd regiment told me.

'I know. I flew over this area three days ago. A Caribou is coming to pick me up with my car tomorrow.'

I preferred a camp bed in the advisers' hut to an air-conditioned trailer. There was no mess, and Jerry, an American sergeant, acted as cook for the group.

Wrapped in an immense N.L.F. flag—about two yards by three —which served as a greatcoat, I went to have a drink with the Vietnamese officers. Two hours of chatting round a wooden table drinking beer or tea, with a blanket stretched across the door behind to protect us from the cold! Captain John McCloskey could speak a little Vietnamese and made visible efforts to improve on it. The *day-uy* didn't speak English too badly. He was hoping to go to a military school in the United States at the end of the year.

'The problem,' John told me, 'is the language. They have to speak more or less fluently to be able to follow the courses, and unfortunately there aren't many bilingual ones.'

'Send those who speak French to the war college in France.'

The joke was not appreciated!

Here relations between the Vietnamese and their advisers appear to be good, even friendly. And this is rare enough to deserve comment!

When I left, I gave the enormous flag back to John.

'I wish I could give it to you, but I'm sorry—it represents an aircraft.'

'What do you mean, an aircraft?'

'All our supplies come from Qui Nhon. They're swamped with work, and naturally there have to be priorities.'

'Who decides on them?

'Essentials come first. But afterwards you can get your delivery more quickly if you bargain with the aircrew: a flag like this one represents a planeload of goods. We can get two planeloads in exchange for a Chinese automatic rifle. Those are the souvenirs they want most. The back areas are crazy to get hold of them.'

They had to go out at six o'clock next morning to patrol along the road and the country round it, hunting for a sniper who liked to pick off planes as they landed or took off. A needle in a haystack! Or almost! I jumped at the chance.

'I'm going with you. I want to take some shots of the first roadblock to prove that I'm only putting the car on a plane because the road really is blocked.'

'No, Michèle, if we have a serious engagement, we may not

get back till after two. You mustn't miss the Caribou that's coming specially for you.'

Though fully dressed down to my socks, and wrapped in two blankets, I could not sleep for the cold. When I heard them go, I got up and went to sit by the fire. Captain Tommy Waugh was there, too.

'I'm going to take a picture of you and send it to my wife to make her a bit jealous!'

That was to be the last photo of me before . . .

About ten o'clock I went to Bong Son with a Vietnamese lieutenant to have Chinese soup. He spoke French, and told me, 'The Vietcong are everywhere. We're expecting a mortar attack any night now.'

Situated in a hollow, the camp was indeed in an ideal position for such an attack.

'What do you think the end of it will be?'

'One way or another, the Vietcong will come out on top.' He said it very simply as if it were something known in advance and which nothing could be done about. It was a question of time, and he was resigned.

At eleven o'clock, when we returned to camp, Tommy was still writing to his wife.

'I think I'll go two or three miles up the road to the north to take some shots of the road-block.'

'You'll meet John and his men. They're on the way back. Be careful, it's dangerous.'

'See you later, I hope!'

One mile farther on, I met the armoured cars.

'Wait ten minutes until No. 1 Company get to the end of the straight stretch.'

The car disappeared under a swarm of children.

'OK! go ahead . . .' the lieutenant called to me as the company came in sight.

'Hello, John! You see, I could have gone with you! You've come back in time.'

'*Be careful!*'

A mile, a mile and a half farther on . . . another company.

'Well, what do you know! A civilian car right here—and white, not khaki . . . *and* a woman driving alone!'

The G.I.s of the First Cavalry insisted on an explanation.

'I'm going two miles farther on to take a picture of the road-block.'

'Do you want a company to go with you?' offered the captain.

'No, I don't want any accident through my fault.'

'Be careful! There are snipers in ambush all around! Another company is following us, so you run the risk of being caught between two fires. Take your picture and come back to camp immediately, if you don't want to be turned into a sieve.'

'I'll be in camp in twenty minutes. 'Bye!'

I left them, not feeling very reassured. A curve, another 500 yards . . . I had a puncture! The first puncture on the whole journey. There was no one at all on the road, all the civilian and military cars had stopped in Bong Son. And 'Victor Charlie' was lurking in the bushes!

14

I am taken Prisoner

A few women, some children. While I was changing the wheel, I tried to make them understand, with my two words of Vietnamese, that I was *bao chi phap*—a French journalist. Two young students helped me, as I was having a bit of difficulty with the wheel. And all the time I was working at it, my mind was racing faster and faster, 'snipers, maybe a hundred yards off, who must surely have seen me already. . . . These villagers, if they aren't armed guerrillas, will surely be Vietcong sympathisers. . . . They'll tip off the others. No one will be able to understand who I am, or what I'm doing here, on a blocked road. . . . Perhaps I'll be taken for a spy. . . .'

The wheel changed, a quick half-turn, burn up the ground! Back to camp for me! I'll take that photo from the plane! To find myself transformed into a target or a sieve doesn't appeal to me at all!

'Can you take us as far as Bong Son?' my two kind helpers asked me. They spoke a little French, very little. They jumped in, and a few hundred yards farther on. . . .

'Quick, stop! Stop!'

I was looking down—I didn't understand.

Five yards ahead stood three guerrillas, two on the right and one on the left. Black, green, and beige pyjamas, trouser legs rolled up, American belts and grenades, Ho Chi Minh sandals, bare heads, guns pointing in our direction, fingers on the trigger. In a tenth of a second, I took it all in. They were getting impatient, for my two 'pals' had trouble opening the door. I leaned over to help them— and a bullet whizzed through the open window into the car. 'Quick, get out, quick!' repeated the two young students, who were still struggling unsuccessfully with the door handle. As I got out, I handed one of the students my passport. He was trembling so much he couldn't open it, and he dropped the papers that were

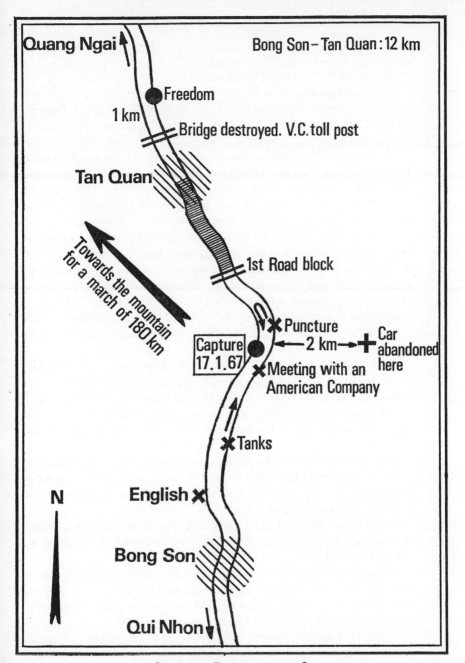

Capture—January 17, 1967

inside. Being caught in the company of a European, perhaps an American, apparently didn't reassure him.

'*Bao chi phap* . . . French journalist.'

To prove my statement I tried to show them my cameras on the back seat. A rustle, and the point of a bayonet in my ribs! Then it dawned on me: through the glass the barrel of the range-finder looked strangely like a weapon.

Then very quickly my arms were tied behind my back, pulled tight enough to hurt me. 'They had the cord all ready!' I thought, 'They were waiting for me, they saw me stop and knew that I would have to turn back.' My mind worked like lightning. 'Everything's got to go right in the first few minutes. Saigon, Nice, the family, Patrick . . . and the Caribou waiting for me in just two hours' time. What with the puncture and the time lost, the Americans must realize by now that something's happened . . . I had the car armourplated, but I haven't brought any vitamins. I thought of it often enough, but with my usual habit of letting things slide. . . .'

So there I was, tied up, a prisoner, with a dozen soldiers round me now, all of them armed, all excited, talking loudly, not knowing what to do.

I felt that I was a problem for them. They have orders to kill anyone who looks like a fighting man. But what could they do with a woman, apparently a non-combatant who said she was French and a journalist? To camouflage the car was even more difficult. It was an ideal target and a landmark which would eventually attract attention.

The bayonet I felt between my ribs terrified me more than the fourteen or fifteen other guns and automatics. There was something barbaric about it, and the man who was holding it seemed more worked up than the others.

I was balanced on a tight-rope. I must be careful not to make any move; the slightest mistake might be fatal. I tried to be calm, to smile. It wasn't easy, but little by little I relaxed.

A combination of circumstances had led up to my presence here this morning. My subconscious perhaps gave a sigh: I was now on 'the other side', I was going to see what it was like and my curiosity, once wakened, struggled against my fear.

I could not get any of them to look me in the eye. I wanted to make them feel that I was calm, to give them the impression that it was all a mistake, but that in any case I wasn't worried. All eyes were riveted on my feet in their military jungle boots. Suddenly I felt sick, with an overwhelming urge to 'be alone'.

'Michèle, you're half-dead with fright!'

When I got into the car again fifteen minutes later, my smile was less strained. Only my left arm was tied, while 'Victor Charlie', holding the other end of the rope, trotted beside the car with his gun still pointed at me, though not the bayonet (Whew!). All the others ran alongside and behind us. I was, so to speak, on the lead! But I was still too tense to laugh at the absurdity of the scene.

'Take it easy, take it easy,' my two students kept repeating.

But my foot trembled on the accelerator, and I couldn't help driving in jerks.

For ten seconds I had a wild hope: 'They're taking me to Bong Son.'

Then I saw a road on the left, a dike through the rice paddy: I was a prisoner all right; there was no more hope, or very little. The Caribou would be waiting for me, ready to leave, as arranged, in an hour. I was obsessed by the thought of that special plane waiting for the rendezvous I couldn't keep, and I was overwhelmed by a feeling of guilt.

More and more women, children, and guerrillas joined our procession. We crossed a number of ditches; every time they had to find planks, and the manœuvre was difficult, for everyone gave different orders, and having my arm tied up didn't make things easier.

An adorable little girl about ten was eating a piece of sugarcane. I held out my hand to her. At first she did not understand at all, then she went and cut a piece for me. I pretended to be stupid— how could you eat a piece of wood like this?

Everybody burst out laughing! It was the first easing of tension, and I felt I had gained a point.

Then I got really stuck in the mud, with the wheels skidding round and round. I tried to explain that we must put some branches under the wheels. So at last they set me free. I got down and helped them lay the brushwood. For the first time the 'Viet-with-the-bayonet' met my eye, gave me a faint smile, then quickly turned his head away.

When we had to cross an open zone I tried to convey to them

by sound and gesture: planes, helicopters, bang, bang, rockets, boom, boom! My feelings at that moment are not hard to imagine. I was on the 'other side' and it was too late to hope for a rescue without casualties.

If an observation plane sighted us, it could mean death, through my fault, not only for me, but for all these women and all these children around me.

With my poncho over the bonnet of the car, a piece of green nylon over the boot, and two palm branches on the roof tied down by the same rope that had tied me, I tore along by the dike.

While I drove—the others were running behind as fast as their legs would carry them—I hunted for my American press card and hid it under the floor mat. I was afraid of being taken for a spy. I would like to have left a note as well, but that was impossible.

After we had gone about a mile and a half, we came up against a ditch too wide to cross, and couldn't drive any farther. So we abandoned the car near a field of sugarcane and continued on foot. I piled my cameras and various belongings into my big travelling bag, and an Air France bag. But I purposely forgot to open the trunk, which held all my military gear, and the bag with my battle dress, canteen, and belt.

Some of the children shouted, '*My! My! My!* O.K. O.K. O.K.!'

A man about thirty-five years old, wearing a North Vietnamese beige uniform with an American automatic stuck in his belt, who now seemed to have taken charge of the operation, made the children keep quiet.

My mind worked rapidly. I tried to think ahead, to foresee everything. I had a notebook with the names of some American officers, and my comments, and the name of a French planter telling an American correspondent who accused him of being pro-Viet: 'Don't forget that we have the same skin.'

All that must be got rid of, but how?

There was only one solution: carrying the bag held tight against my chest, and looking unconcerned, I tore out the pages one by one and chewed them conscientiously, before swallowing them or spitting them out reduced to a pulp.

'Beer or Coca Cola?'

So I was still living in the American age! We had stopped at a

Vietnamese house: walls of dried mud and a straw roof. Rice, pâté, fish and hot tea for the three prisoners. We were three because my unfortunate hitch-hikers were also being detained.

The guerrillas were grouped round a table, the women near the fire. It was dark, and a lot of people had gathered in the open door. I wasn't quite sure what attitude to take. One soldier showed me his bayonet, saying very proudly '*Phap*'. Yes, it's my pal of a little while ago! His eyes are no longer throwing out sparks. He's relaxed and even smiles at me.

The leader paid our host for the meal and the Coca Cola—and this wasn't the last time he did so!

'They were trying to bluff you,' American officials told me after I was released. 'You were a newspaperwoman.'

No. Not just one hour after my capture. They'd not had time to adopt a policy towards me. They acted courteously, as if it were the usual and the natural thing for them to do.

We set off again in Indian file. The children and women who had surrounded us from the beginning disappeared after one of my guards had shouted at them. We marched for a mile and a half, perhaps more, and it was about three o'clock when we came to a house where I was to spend the whole afternoon.

The room was rectangular in shape with a bed of planks on each side of the ancestral shrine. I sat down on the edge of one of the beds, with my possessions scattered round me—cameras, films, photographic material, but also a flowered bikini and a miniskirt for the beach!

The other bed was covered with women and babies. And in the space between, a crowd of people were milling about almost non-stop.

I was the attraction, like a cinema, or some such curiosity.

'Keep calm, Michèle,' I told myself. 'Smile, try to hide your feet under the bed, for too many fingers are pointing at your military boots.'

Twenty times perhaps they rummaged through my bags. Each time a list in French and one in Vietnamese. More than twenty times, too, I had to write on a piece of paper:

'I am Michèle Ray, a journalist. I came from Qui Nhon on the main road.'

The whole afternoon the leader sat on the end of the bed, his legs
KH

crossed, chin in his hands, watching me. What was he thinking? His steady gaze embarrassed me.

It must have been four o'clock. An observation plane had been circling above us for the last two hours. Was it looking for me? I doubted it, in view of the lapse of time. In any case, it's too late now, Jo! The car is camouflaged, and I'm inside a house. Not a chance of being spotted.

The two Vietnamese students were set free. As they left they called to me, 'Good luck!' and 'That's life!' I was suddenly very tired, but I also had a tremendous urge to box their ears.

Wearing black pyjamas and a belt hung with grenades—American, of course—arms crossed, and a fiercely determined expression, a woman partisan came in and planted herself in front of me.

'A fine figure of a woman! I wouldn't like to find myself in her hands, all alone!'

'She's been looking for you for a month. We want to know what we don't know,' one of my guards said to me in very bad French.

I went hot all over, and I had to sit on my hands to hide their trembling.

Why were they looking for me? What had I done? They had something on me, but what? Trial and sentence. . . . For twenty minutes we had a deaf-and-dumb conversation.

'All right, let's get down to it. This woman has been following me for a month?'

'Yes. To find out what we don't know.'

'But what?'

'What we don't know.'

I made signs with my hands. We began again from the beginning.

I had the feeling I was going mad. Everyone had stopped talking and was watching us. It seemed to be a very important and serious moment. I was balanced on a tight-rope once again. And this woman who disturbed me with her grim, withdrawn manner—not a smile, nothing. It was right out of Kafka, and I wanted to cry.

Suddenly a little boy made signs to me, pointed to his pockets and turned them inside out. They wanted to search me! Nothing more than that!

I'll never know what they meant by 'She's been following you for a month.' Come to that, I didn't want to know any longer. I was alive! It was enough!

The atmosphere immediately became more relaxed. No strip-tease. The woman was laughing as she went through all my pockets: my money, my Vietnamese press card. Then they naturally had to draw up more lists—several copies of them, of course—their paperwork was beginning to get on my nerves. At eight o'clock another character appeared.

'I'm a Communist professor. We must get going and have a chat somewhere else.'

He must have been about twenty years old, slender, with fine features and the hands of a child.

What exactly did he mean, 'have a chat somewhere else'?

When I stood up at last, I felt giddy. I was a good head taller than any of them, and I felt like Alice among the Lilliputians!

The leader, who until then had not stopped watching me, went outside for a few minutes and then came back with two tins of sweetened condensed milk. Smiling at me, he put them in my bag. The women came up to touch me—it was their way of saying, 'Goodbye'. There were five of us who left.

I headed the march beside the young professor, followed by a N.L.F. agent with a square head and a magnificent set of teeth. I immediately christened him, 'White Teeth'. And finally, two young porters with rifles over their shoulders. They carried my big, black bag slung on a pole between them. Later on, our porters changed fairly often. But they were always the same type: young, long-haired, smiling easily, and they were all 'The Beatles' to me. As they would never tell me their real names, the nickname sticks in my mind to this day.

We were going back the same way. I tried to get my bearings, and it was easy enough.

'Hullo! The car has disappeared!'

'Covered with earth,' they explained.

Not much chance of them finding even a trace of me. As far as Saigon was concerned, I had vanished into thin air. I had only myself to rely on now, my ingenuity, my luck, and more than anything, the good will of these Vietcong gentlemen, of 'Victor Charlie', as the G.I.s say—'my friends', as I was to call them when I was set free.

'You sing.'

It was not a question; it was almost an order. I was scared. I didn't know any songs, and I can't sing.

'Quick, Michèle. Think of something.'

Alouette, A la claire fontaine, Au clair de la lune, Frère Jacques—the latter as a duet with the professor, the only one who could chatter a bit in French. And at the end, to crown it all, the *Marseillaise*. Not to be outdone, my guards thundered out some songs, which all sounded nationalistic, if not downright revolutionary.

Then the artillery began shelling from the direction of 'English'. Last night they'd stopped me sleeping, and I'd cursed them. Now we all began to sing at the top of our voices to cover the sound of the guns.

I started giggling hysterically—I couldn't stop myself. My friends must be imagining me dead, and here I was, under fire from American mortars, singing with 'Victor Charlie'. But he was prepared for it, proof against this kind of inconvenience, which is a daily occurrence for him. Every five yards at the most, often every yard, there was a foxhole beside the path that ran along the dike, in the middle of the rice field.

The shells were falling closer. Quick, everyone into a hole, about five feet deep. You had to duck right down, to protect your head. I was thinking all the time about Saigon, where they must know about me by now. I could imagine their comments.

'If only I'd captured her, what a situation!'

'If she wasn't killed to begin with, she'll soon have the Vietcong in her pocket. Trust her for that.'

'Poor Michèle, under a B-52 bombardment, in the hottest spot. But one small consolation: I'm the only one with photographs of her.'

'Jesus Christ! I must go and find her!'

As for the officials: 'No search can be made for her.'

Tuesday, January 17, 1967
Nine hours after my capture, United Press International released the news. The report was based on information from villagers in the neighbourhood of Bong Son, who had seen 'a young white woman kidnapped by the Vietcong'.

15

Hell

Rain, marching, singing, foxholes, gunfire—close, too close!—one thing followed another—all in rapid succession.

'Are you from this province, or from the North? From Hanoi? Did you come on foot over the Ho Chi Minh Trail?'

I was not being grilled myself any longer, I was even bold enough to ask some questions. There was a lot of talk and laughter.

'You gay, you brave!'

Gay, I agree, since whether I liked it or not, I had to sing. But why brave? What time was it? Perhaps two o'clock in the morning. The fact that I didn't wear a watch always amazed them, for to their mind it was a status symbol.

Another house, and me sitting once again on another bed. In groups of three or four the combatants arrived.

'Communists, Hanoi,' the professor (explained for my benefit), his voice full of admiration, and his eyes bright.

Most of them wore beige, with knapsacks on their backs—not very full ones—belts hung with grenades, and automatic rifles. Each man in turn would plant himself in front of me, make a speech, shake my hand vigorously and grin broadly.

This went on for more than an hour.

'What has come over them? What are they saying? They look as if they're congratulating me, but for what?'

A woman sat down beside me, took me in her arms, and rocked me as if I were a baby. It was the first time I had been comforted since the beginning of the afternoon, and it went to my heart.

There was one tall young soldier in black pyjamas, armed, with a profile like a Greek coin, and so handsome that I couldn't take my eyes off him. He was playing enthusiastically with two little boys, teasing them, hugging them, cuddling them. He was the ideal picture of youth, strength, virility, and self-confidence, with a touching hint of boyishness. It was hard for me to realize that these were the notorious Vietcong, who had existed in my mind as a vague black mass, shifting, silent, and—more than anything else—impersonal. Yet here they were—real women, real children, a real man who laughed and joked before going off to make war, and perhaps to die—who knows where?

For my second meal there was rice and fish pickled in brine. It was hard to swallow, but I was hungry after the long day. By now it must have been four o'clock in the morning.

'You must try out the shelter for tomorrow,' the professor told me.

In procession, paraffin lamps in our hands, we walked about 100 yards from the house. From the outside I could see nothing. Everything was camouflaged, and a bush hid the entrance. With the help of gestures, they showed me how to slide down into the dug-out. With arms above your head, drop feet first down the vertical shaft, then slide along the connecting trench, still feet first and wriggling on your back, till you finally reach the hidden shelter.

The shelter measured roughly six feet in length by three by three. The props were of coconut-wood, but the rest was not cemented; it was made of earth. The Vietnamese could get down into it in five seconds, but for me, even after one, two, three tries, it still took half a minute. My height did not exactly help.

There wasn't much left of the night when I got back to my bed of planks, with a block of wood for a pillow, and a piece of matting for a blanket. I was frozen; in fact, apart from the American bombings, I suffered more from the cold than anything during my captivity.

At seven in the morning the bombardment began in earnest. Everyone rushed for the shelter. I forgot to lift my arms, and I had to come out and start again! There were nine of us crouching side by side!

For ventilation, there were only two bamboo canes, about two inches in diameter, whose tips were camouflaged outside. Inside, total darkness. Impossible to light a candle which would use up some of the oxygen. For two hours, artillery fire, aircraft and helicopters. I found it difficult to breathe, I was frightened . . . 'What am I doing here!'

Patrick, my parents, everyone must know. I could imagine how upset they were.

During a lull in the bombing, the shelter was opened for five

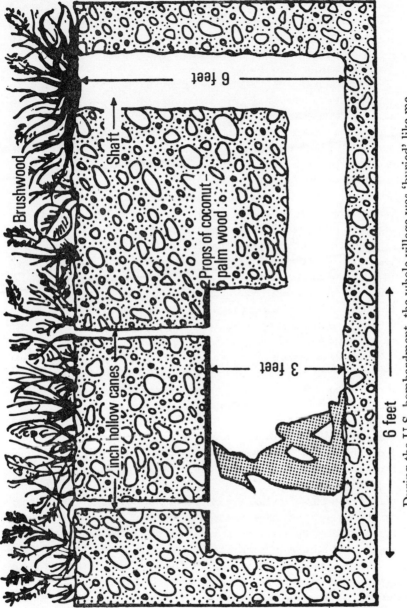

During the U.S. bombardment, the whole village was 'buried' like me

minutes and five of the soldiers went out. Were they going to fight? There were four of us left: two Beatles, the Communist professor, and me.

'Lie down and sleep, to forget the time,' the professor advised me. Forget the time! Easy enough to say.

How could I sleep? The ground shook, and the shocks were unbearably violent. We heard the sound of the jets as they dived to the attack, then we had to wait for a few hellish seconds before we knew that this time the bomb was not for us. It was hell indeed. Lying full length was the worst. It seemed to me that sitting down, my head between my legs, I'd be better protected. Suddenly I felt a small hand in mine. It was the professor's. If I was frightened, he was frightened, too. Human contact reassured us a little, but not much. The worst was not really the bombs exploding but the helicopters and the roar of their rockets as they were launched.

I could visualize the pilots pushing the buttons, I could hear their jokes. Two months ago I had been filming them, and it all came back to my mind in clear detail—I didn't imagine then that one day I'd be 'down below', that I would be the target. All the figures whirled about in my head: 200 tons of bombs dropped daily on South Vietnam, 100 tons of napalm. Today it seemed to me that they were concentrating all of it right here, on top of me!

I was covered with dirt; I took off my sweater. I was panting, it was getting more and more difficult to breathe. I moved closer to the bamboo canes, stretched out full length, sat up, stretched out again, tried to block my ears.

Suddenly bombs were exploding on top of us, and rockets, and I was terrified that a grenade might be hurled right into the dug-out. I couldn't stand any more—I was going crazy! I felt I was being buried alive, and a wave of claustrophobia surged over me. I'd die if I had to, but I wanted to die in the open. I crawled towards the exit. The professor pulled me back and tried to explain to me that up there was certain death. He took my hand again, and at every new explosion he squeezed it a little tighter. I began to cry with anger and fright, with weariness and utter exhaustion.

I knew that if the G.I.s found our hiding place, we would get a grenade thrown down on us, and if by chance we happened on a 'greenhorn' it would be a Beatle's turn to hurl up one of the grenades he wore on his belt. But my fate would be the same either way. I'd

Letter written on one of the back pages of Robert Merle's
The Island, by my first professor

be blown to bits by an American grenade whether it was thrown by an alert G.I., or by one of my Vietcong buddies. Four hours, five hours, how many hours since I've been shut up in this tomb? Time has no more meaning. I unbuttoned my shirt and loosened my trousers. I simply had to breathe. A vice seemed to tighten round my head, and then I vomited. The stench was unbearable. I didn't even care about the bombing any more. Stretched out on my back, I began to lose consciousness. The professor put his arms around my legs and leaned his head against my knees. In a final moment of awareness, I saw the expression on the G.I.s faces if they found me dead in that position! And what would the papers say?

When I came to myself again, all was quiet. There was a gleam of daylight at the end of the tunnel, and the air being fresher did me more good than anything. The professor was still beside me, smiling, attentive, full of sympathy. What time was it? Six-thirty in the evening. Almost twelve hours in that hole—and I get claustrophobia in a lift!

Instead of green pyjamas, the professor was wearing a white shirt and blue trousers. Now I understood why he had been breathing heavily a while back at the height of the bombing: he was changing his clothes, for fear of being taken prisoner. He had turned himself into a simple villager. Beside me now he held a sheet of paper from an exercise book in his hand and a pen:

'I want a letter from you, in memory of our holding hands during the bombing, in memory of our fear.'

'Tomorrow. I'm not even strong enough to hold a pen.'

'No. Now.'

And feeling like a little girl, I obeyed. I wrote the souvenir letter. I don't remember exactly what I said, but I really think it was almost a love letter—brotherly love—because his hand had stood for human warmth and life under that avalanche of bombs.

We crawled up and out of the hole. What had become of the women, the children, the soldiers? But no, all those I was afraid of seeing dead or wounded were there waiting for me.

They joked and laughed. They thought it was funny—and also perhaps a little touching—that fate had forced a European woman to share their suffering and their fear.

There were no wounded, no dead. They were getting used to living like moles or rats. Like us, they had all gone underground.

Two houses had been napalmed and had just stopped burning, and all around us were bomb craters. I had not been dreaming. We had been the centre of an attack. But I must stick to the evidence: it did not look to me as though this attack, which had lasted all day, had served any purpose at all. What? Everyone around me, villagers and soldiers alike, were relaxed, joking and laughing. The professor explained that they were teasing each other about how they'd reacted to the attack and how fast they'd reached their shelters or their various firing posts.

More rice and pickled fish. I ate it but I couldn't keep it down. They were worried and made me inhale from a little bottle of Chinese medicine—camphor, probably. Their concern was very touching. But, then, I was in the mood to be emotional about anything.

As on the previous night, there was a march-past of fighting men and a lot of handshaking and speeches before we left to 'have a chat' elsewhere. The shelling began again. For half an hour we had to take shelter in the family hide-out. It was not really a shelter, just a dug-out, lined with cocoa-palm wood. In it gathered women, children, villagers, cambos (political commissioners), and soldiers. They all wanted me to sing. Stretched out, with his feet against the wall and his little roll of rice around his neck, the man who seemed to be in charge of the village listened dreamily.

During a lull in the firing, we set out—the same group as the night before. I sang at the top of my lungs! At last I could breathe! I'd never be able to get enough oxygen into my lungs. A prisoner? Yes, but I was surrounded by warm solicitude, I was alive, and it was marvellous! I had escaped from hell!

Another house, another bed of planks, another shelter, another bombardment. The same fear, too. I was still being sick. The second day was strangely like the first.

Wednesday, January 18, 1967
At noon Zalin Grant, of *Time* magazine, reached Te Duc, (Bong Son-English), which I had left an hour before my capture.

He had practically no information about me. He knew nothing about the special Caribou plane which had arrived at 2 o'clock and had waited for more than two hours for me.

Fortunately, Grant found an old friend, Colonel George Casey, commanding the Third Brigade of the First Cavalry.

'Operation orders have already been drawn up. The First
Cavalry can do nothing for Michèle,' he told him. 'Besides, the
M.A.C.V. has sent out word to do nothing. But if you can get
any valid information and persuade the Vietnamese to give you a
company, come to me with a plan and I will help you.'

Thursday, January 19, 1967

Grant, the only one in the press corps who spoke Vietnamese,
managed to make friends with Lieutenant Colonel Nguyen Long,
commanding the 42nd Regiment of A.R.V.N. All day long they
questioned prisoners, captured the night before during the bomb
attack. To gain their confidence (piastres not always being
effective), Grant said he was 'a Frenchman searching for his
wife'.

Henri Huet, a Frenchman working for the Associated Press
(he was awarded the Robert Capa prize), arrived in 'English' the
same day. Christian Simonpiétri, my childhood friend, also
turned up, and finally, Alain Raymond, who represented the
A.F.P. and all my friends from the office in Saigon.

With the willing help of the pilots, as soon as they realized that
the men were searching for me as friends rather than as newspaper
men, a number of reconnaissance flights by helicopter took place
along the road.

Towards evening, the correspondents found a secret agent of the
national police. The agent, a mercenary, carried with him some
American handbills offering rewards for pilots who had been
shot down. Condemned to death by the Vietcong, the agent had
always managed to escape by never sleeping more than twice
in the same house. In return for money he was persuaded to
point out the position of my car.

'But you'll get more information if you could go and look for
yourself. Then you can question the people in the neighbourhood,' he told all the correspondents.

It was Thursday evening, too, when some Vietnamese soldiers
handed over to the American advisers of the 42nd Regiment and
their senior officer, Major Porter, several documents taken from a
Vietcong captured during the day. In a notebook, after some
information about the installations of the First Cavalry Division
at 'English', was a paragraph:

'A European woman has been captured today near Cau No Nuoc Mam (the Nuoc Man bridge). She says she is a French journalist working for a French magazine, but we suspect her of working for the American Army.'

My friends then decided to have leaflets printed certifying that I really was a journalist and was not working for the Americans.

It was Major Jones, P.I.O. of the First Cavalry, who undertook to have the leaflets dropped, with the co-operation of the Service of Propaganda.

16

Dreams are Necessary

Friday, January 20, 1967
At last I was able to keep down my breakfast of rice and fish.

Before returning to his village, the professor insisted that I wrote down the words of the *Marseillaise* for him. He wanted to teach them to his pupils. The G.I.s will be surprised when one day they land in a ruined village and hear the French national anthem! These people wanted me to dress like a Vietnamese, so a tailor arrived and took my measurements. The length of the trousers amused everyone. Afterwards, I slept, rested, or read under the attentive, curious, but not hostile, eyes of the villagers.

> *Friday, January 20, 1967*
> Now that they knew the exact position of the car, the journalists obtained the services of eight 'Huey' helicopters from Colonel Casey and a company of seventy-eight men from Colonel Long.

I'd often passed through villages when I was following American or Vietnamese operations—and the men were never visible. Here, they're present and alive—not only soldiers, but peasants, too. But one day troops will come; that will mean evacuation and then there will be only women and children left—as everywhere else, for that matter. For the men the choice is inevitable—they must go 'to the other side'—whether they want to or not.

'Good morning, Madame.'

This is a new professor, a Communist too, and moreover a professor of Communism. In the liberated zones the N.L.F. takes charge of the education of children and adults. The latter also receive political education.

The professor is to stay with me on the mountain for six days. He is small, neither fat nor thin, with glasses, a green pyjama-suit, and an intelligent forehead under his Basque beret. He is a native of the

province of Binh Dinh, where he studied at the French school in
Qui Nhon before teaching at the University of Hanoi from 1955 to
1962. He was Vietminh under the French, who imprisoned him in
Huê. His sister is a professor of Russian at the Hanoi Polytechnic
School. The letters they write to each other take at least three
months to arrive. He gave gave me her address.

'If you go to Hanoi, promise to go and see her,' he said to me on
leaving. At present he is acting as interpreter to the district head of
the National Liberation Front. In his impeccable French he told
me, 'We have to hold you for a certain time.'

A certain time, according to precedent, can mean anything from
three days to six months!

'We must know who you really are, and because of American
operations, our communications are fairly difficult. You are going
up into the mountains tonight. You will be safer there than here.
We wish we could give you all the food you need, but this is war:
we will do the best we can. Consider yourself a guest, not a prisoner.
We must also come to a decision about your wish to return to
Hanoi on foot. We find it very courageous of you, and we admire
you very much.'

Hanoi! Hanoi on foot! There must have been some misunder-
standing. But when? Most likely with the first professor, who spoke
French so badly. Now I see the reason for all that handshaking
during the last few days. I wanted to say something, to try to explain.
But it was too late.

'Write to your family, to your friends, to Patrick, that you are in
good health and perhaps on the way to Hanoi.'

I wonder what became of those letters.

I've changed my personality. No more beige trousers and
American sky-blue shirt. I'm wearing my new black pyjama-suit,
made to measure, a cone-shaped hat, and here I am—transformed
into a Vietnamese. The only odd note is my army boots. I wanted
to pay the tailor, but it was all a 'present'.

There were more embraces and handshakes as I got ready to
leave for the mountain.

Though White Teeth has left us, Lynx Eye has replaced him.
With a piercing and mischievous eye, a crew-cut, and one tuft
of hair which stuck forward like a finger pointing, he is our guide.
He knows all the trails. After the rice field, we walked along

a little stream—my feet were in water for an hour! After that came the forest and then the mountain.

And silence? No! Lynx Eye turned the transistor that was slung across his shoulders on at full blast. And he was always searching for animal tracks with his torch . . . evidently he wants to reinforce our diet.

I smiled as I recalled the comment of one violently anti-American newspaper: 'The G.I.s go to war with their M.16 in one hand and their transistor in the other.' Here it's just the same, except that there's propaganda instead of Nancy Sinatra and 'Boots'.

All night long we walked through the jungle—uphill, downhill, then up and down again. We rested for about ten minutes every hour. Now it's more open country—it's the first time I've seen a rice field in the mountains. It must have been just before six and still dark when we arrived, exhausted, at a house just as the daily ritual of tooth-brushing was going on.

Saturday, January 21, 1967

At eight o'clock a campaign was launched for the recovery of my car. A battalion of A.R.V.N., coming from Tam Quan and heading south over route No. 1, acted as a blocking force while the war correspondents and *their* company landed in helicopters in the paddy, quite near the car.

A few shots were fired by snipers as the helicopters landed. But Captain Robert Fraley, the company's American adviser, decided not to hunt for them. They had come to find the car, question the peasants, and discover some trace of me.

The Dauphine was 200 yards from where they landed, camouflaged in a field of sugarcane, and booby-trapped with a howitzer shell and an American grenade, the latter attached to the wheel by a string. The explosion would surely have killed anyone within twenty yards, if the car had been shifted before the fuse had been disconnected.

A woman told them that the Vietcong had taken me to the mountain but did not intend to kill me; that they would set me free when they had established exactly who I was.

At that moment a Vietcong opened fire on a Government soldier, who returned it. When the exchange was over, three Vietcong were dead, and another had been captured.

Then a strange manœuvre began. Because the key had been removed from the car and the wheels were jammed, the journalists and soldiers set off to carry the car across the rice paddy, over little bridges and dikes.

'We were still at it when night fell,' Christian told me later. 'Right in the middle of the Vietcong zone! We could have been shot down like flies. I imagine they were too engrossed watching this ridiculous performance, and couldn't believe their eyes!'

During the weeks that followed their return to Saigon, the correspondents took it in turns to come back every two or three days, in the hope of getting further information. Knowing that I was in the hands of the N.L.F., that I had not been 'stupidly' shot on the road, reassured them to a certain extent. And like me, they thought, or at least hoped, that I might be freed during the Têt truce.

We stayed in the same area, right up until the day I was released. The faintest sound of a helicopter or a plane sent us scurrying into the jungle on foot, trying to hide ourselves beside a mountain stream or in a hollow in the rocks, perhaps the lair of a tiger.

For some reason my memory of these days is confused, with just a few facts which come back to my mind, for no particular reason. Even though I began my diary again and kept it fairly regularly, I lost a day. According to my record I was freed on a Sunday. In actual fact it was a Monday, February 6. That made twenty days in all with 'the other side'.

Somewhere in Binh Dinh province with the N.L.F. . . . . January
For the first time I'm sad. I am passing through a valuable and thrilling experience, but I don't know what the end of it will be. Perhaps I am depressed because the professor, the only one who speaks French, is leaving tomorrow morning. This sector seems to be a sort of no-man's-land.

I think I am on the border of Binh Dinh and Quang Ngai, the frontier between No. 1 tactical zone—the Marines—and No. 2 zone—where the First Cavalry operates. So far there have not been any joint operations.

The rice paddy, laid out in terraces, extends over two or three square miles. There is no village, but a house—with the inevitable

LH

dug-out—and a family about every 500 yards. The first three days were relatively quiet. The only bombing came at irregular intervals from the Seventh Fleet. White Teeth has come back with a young girl, 'Co,' whose duty it is to cook for our little group. The Beatles, with their easy, infectious laughter, come and go incessantly. They also act as messengers. A minimum of two reports a day are sent out. Wrapped in school paper and sealed with rice paste, they are sent off . . . where? The paperwork is getting on my nerves. I know that the messages are about me. What on earth can they be reporting? Every action, every gesture I make?

So as not to be too much of a burden on the families who lodge us, we spend two or three days with one, and two or three days with another. We carry our rice with us, in packets round our necks. We haven't enough rice bowls left, so there are always two sittings.

We put a wooden tray on the ground—or one made from an old napalm container—and around it we arrange the bowls, the chopsticks and the dish of rice. A soup made of some kind of herb—a cure for everything, the professor explains—makes the rice go down more easily.

From time to time we have a little manioc or some other root vegetable, and very occasionally fish from the rice field—or some chicken. But one chicken feeds a whole family for about ten days! That means very little in the stomach for each person. White Teeth pays for all these extras, and I cannot help making certain comparisons.

I don't just eat now because I'm hungry. I'm even beginning to enjoy it. The little cravings I had at first for Coca Cola and hot cakes —what a disgrace for a Frenchwoman!—have disappeared. For drink and dessert combined we have boiled water and green tea at every meal. My chief difficulty, though, is not getting used to the food, but squatting on my heels to eat it, Vietnamese-fashion. They took pity on me, and laughing, gave me a block of wood.

Every day we see troops on the move—porters or soldiers. There are a few women among them, loaded down with enormous sacks. One girl in particular, very slender and small, with hair cut short, who looks like a shepherdess.

'A nurse,' they told me.

Camouflaged by thick branches fastened on their knapsacks,

with others on their hats and their weapons, and coming silently towards me from a distance, they look like moving bushes.

Just an army of peasants in pyjamas and rubber sandals, but a well-organized army, with weapons that aren't makeshift any longer. Often two or three soldiers leave the column and stop in a house to rest for several days. Some of them are North Vietnamese, others natives of this province.

One of them cut himself with a knife. I tried to disinfect the wound with the few things I had, but he was a bit of a coward. I teased him gently.

'Yes, it's true. I'm afraid of being wounded, of being taken prisoner. I'm afraid of suffering.'

'And of death?'

'No, it is good to die for a cause, to die like a hero, perhaps.'

The professor, who acts as interpreter for us all, also translated some pamphlets for me and the *Front-Line Bulletin* printed in Bong Son for the provinces of Quang Ngai and Binh Dinh. I remember, in particular, the story of Trong Thi Dao, a young partisan girl of twenty who, with the help of three other girls, her friends—two of whom were killed—stopped the advance of an American column of *2,000 soldiers*. Dao took part in more than 200 battles. I protested:

'You're intelligent, you can't believe such rubbish.'

But the professor replied:

'We must have dreams. Do you know why the "puppet" troops fight so badly? They have no dreams.'

I'm learning, I'm getting used to their terminology: *Khieu-Ty*, imperialist lackeys, puppet government, puppet troops; *Morane** for observation plane; *good inhabitants,* for non-Communist villagers ('American imperialists kill good inhabitants.')

The name *Vietcong* makes them furious.

'Don't call us Vietcong any more. *Vietcong* means Vietnamese Communist. We are not all Communists. Many of us are nationalists, and all the political parties are represented in the N.L.F.'

Every day at eleven o'clock, I listen to the broadcast in French from Radio Hanoi. I am no longer living by Saigon time, but by Hanoi time—one hour's difference.

'Four hundred thousand Americans in the South; 108,000 killed,' declares the woman announcer.

* Name of old French observation planes (F.A.C. the Americans call them).

'So are there only 292,000 Americans left now, or is each dead man immediately replaced?'

This problem seems to worry them a lot.

The Army Theatre arrived from Hanoi—a dozen men and women. Performances can only be given where it's easy to get out and where there are plenty of foxholes and shelters.

'One of the actors is a friend of mine,' the professor told me. 'He's an artist from Hué, where we were prisoners together under the French. They were all captured at Phu-Cat. 'But,' he added with a touch of pride in his voice, 'with the help of the local population, they were able to escape.'

I never had the courage to tell him that I'd seen them all, about two weeks before, in the prisoners' camp at Pleiku. Nor did I tell him that 'his artist friend' had given me a painting, left behind in my car.

I got the impression that they were perhaps even more surprised than the Americans by my trip from Ca Mau to Bong Son.

'And you've never been stopped before?'

I drew them a detailed road map and pointed out the sections controlled by the N.L.F. I felt that I was back with General Collins!

'Perhaps we've lost a little ground,' the professor admitted, 'but we still hold the strategic and tactical initiative.'

To my question 'Is this a defeat for you?' he reacted violently: 'No! And in any case, we are all determined to fight on to the end, to victory. Ground won results in non-Communist villagers being sent off to concentration camps, far away from their bombed houses. The imperialists may call them "defectors," but they are still on our side and continue to pass back information. Their hearts are not on "the other side"; for them the enemy is the Americans who bomb them, who force them to leave their villages, and everything they possess. Their husbands or their brothers have stayed on our side.'

Our political conversations have no hint of brain-washing about them. It's usually between two games of cards—our favourite pastime—that we get on to the subject.

Lynx Eye is anti-cards. He prefers to go on studying, working, or singing the praises of Nguyen Van Troi—the people's hero who tried to kill McNamara. All the Vietnamese in the N.L.F. have to learn about his life, like a lesson.

'There are rumours of clashes between the regular army of the

tiểu đội 13
(section)
    tiểu đội
        tiểu đội

trung đội ≈ 40
(peloton)

Compagnie   đại đội
           120

bataillon tiểu đoàn
          360

brigade   trung đoàn
           1080

> 3000 liên đội

(division) sư đoàn
        ≈ 40.000

Explanation of a Vietcong division by the professor

North and the National Liberation Front,' I ventured. 'Would you accuse them of using you, in a sort of way, as pawns?'

The professor hesitated, then said, 'The bombings only serve to unite us all.' And he changed the subject by explaining to me the organization of a North Vietnamese division, consisting of 10,000 men.

. . . January

The three soldiers in the house today were, I think, part of the Second Division to judge by the sign 2D at the top of one of their passes and on their sacks.

I also remembered that Major Porter had told me at Bong Son, 'The Vietcong 22nd Regiment and the North Vietnamese Second division are in the north.' A very important colonel was also said to be in that sector. As he apparently wears no badges of rank or other distinguishing marks, I may have passed this famous colonel on the road.

The majority of the soldiers, about eighty per cent, must be between twenty and twenty-two years old. Their gaiety, their jokes, and their good humour fascinate me. After two hours spent in a relaxed atmosphere, talking and joking, one of them will suddenly become serious.

'Perhaps you'll think badly of us. We shouldn't laugh. This is war.'

He's obviously apologizing, afraid that I may not understand their deep suffering. I'm always very touched by it.

'But, on the contrary,' I replied, 'I think it's wonderful!'

It seems to me that their laughter helps to explain their strength, their confidence and their endurance. The nicest part of the day is certainly the evening. Then everyone relaxes.

The houses are all alike—one large room approximately nine by fifteen or sixteen feet. In one corner, the hearth. Opposite, at right angles, two plank beds. The entrance is closed at night by two large round trays of plaited straw that are used in the daytime for drying rice.

The whole family in one bed—father, mother and children. I sleep in the second bed with Co. And in hammocks slung all over the place are Lynx Eye and White Teeth, the Beatles, and any soldiers passing through. In addition, there are always two or three commissioners or *cambos*, stopping for the night there before going on their way. About twenty people altogether, as well as hens and chickens.

I may be brave, but I have always been afraid—of poultry! It used to be impossible to make me pick up a feathered head of any kind. Here I am becoming calmer and more resigned to it!

Though I wear socks at night, the cold often keeps me from sleeping. The father of the family slips on an old military overcoat, a souvenir of the French army, then he distributes garlic drops—vitamins. I don't mind that, but the smell upsets me.

By the light of a kerosene lamp, sitting cross-legged on *my* bed, three or four of us play cards. No one likes to lose, and we all try to cheat. I have taken to the Vietnamese games: hearts, like *belote*, and *cam len*, a kind of mock poker without stakes. I am so enthusiastic that they have nicknamed me *Cam len* ('grabber'). For me the game is complicated because I have to call the bets in Vietnamese.

The people who live in neighbouring houses, although some way off, come to watch our 'battles'—in particular a little old woman, knee-high to a grasshopper, all wrinkled and toothless. She is my great friend. She repeats after me:

'Good day, Madame! How are you? Very well, thank you . . .'

I learned yesterday that her three sons—Vietminh—had been killed by the French.

'I thought all Frenchwomen were fat and gloomy. You are slender and gay like us.'

'Your journey is dangerous,' they tell me, 'Don't forget that the Vietcong were Vietminh. The fact that you are a Frenchwoman does not protect you completely.'

All the people around me have been Vietminh. I never found the slightest trace of bitterness in them: that's all over, the page has been turned.

The professor often talks to me with warm affection of Monsieur and Madame Bouleran, his teachers at the French college. He admires them enormously.

At night even after the lamp is turned out, Lynx Eye continues to let his transistor roar: propaganda, news, stage plays—all in Vietnamese!

Because the noise stupefies me, because I can't sleep, because I think too much, I often feel like crying.

Without asking my permission, they have sorted out my possessions, leaving me as little as possible: soap, toothpaste, a battered book, slippers, a piece of American parachute for a blanket, a hammock (donated by the N.L.F.), a nylon cover for the hammock when it rains—'American nylon is no good, the nylon of the first Resistance Movement at the time of the French was much stronger'—a shirt, and always my tins of concentrated milk. I carry it all in a black canvas knapsack. My money I keep in my pocket. For the rest, White Teeth has given me a list, and a receipt. He is responsible for everything both to the N.L.F. and to me. When we have to leave in a hurry because the helicopters or the Moranes are getting near, the peasants make themselves responsible for burying my belongings *somewhere*.

A Beatle has found my false plaits. For several seconds I read in his eyes 'She has scalped someone!'

The little boy of the house, a scamp of ten years old, a street urchin Vietnamese style, promptly puts them on and mimics me: 'I am Co, Michèle.' Then looking me up and down, he asks, 'What is the difference between a French girl and an American one?'

The professor tries to explain to him. 'Really, I don't know. For me they're just the same!'

17

I go Blind

Friday, January 27

Before he left, the professor gave me some medicines which the Front had turned over to him for my use—vitamin B_{12}, atropine, morphine, bandages, syringe—all of them of French, Chinese, or American make. I still had four American tablets for malaria—one a week. He apologized:

'I must go back to my pupils. If you are still here for the Têt, it is possible they may send me back.'

'Your pupils must hate me for taking you away from them.'

'Perhaps, on the contrary, they're delighted! An extra holiday!'

'Is schooling the same with you as it is under the South Vietnamese Government?'

'No, we have compulsory education in Hanoi. And a more concentrated curriculum. We gain a year.'

'Are you paid for it?'

'An allocation of rice and 300 piastres a month: that is an absolute minimum. I also work as a medical supervisor. When the war is over, I shall go back to teaching at the university.'

He was going to leave, and I had a thousand more questions to ask him. I was suddenly desperate to go on talking French. One question I just had to ask:

'Do you think the Front is holding me until they can make contacts and set me free for ransom—money, perhaps, or medicines? I am beginning to get worked up . . . I'm a journalist, and I won't accept any sort of freedom on terms.'

'I don't really know what the leaders have in mind, but I think I can safely say "no". I asked you for the address of the French Sisters at Qui Nhon* to let them know that you were with us, and in good health. We are poor, but proud. Very proud, too, to have a journalist sharing our life.'

* They never received any message.

I wanted to believe him, but that night when I could not sleep, I asked myself too many questions, and I began to cry and felt terribly alone. Everyone was so concerned that I began to feel more like a great friend, than just a visitor. But the very fact of thinking 'You're a prisoner', however much they gild the cage, is upsetting in itself, and makes me want to escape.

And this uncertainty about my future . . . I've taken a paragraph from *The Island* by Robert Merle, the only book I've got with me, and copied it into the front of my diary:

Don't think any more, accept the present, get rid of your fears. This obsession about the future that white men have. We are alive, and that should be enough for us.

I must learn to live from day to day, but thinking of Patrick and of my family, who are probably desperate with anxiety, undermines my morale.

I decided that if I get back one day I'll write to Robert Merle: 'Your book has often helped me enormously. Thank you.'

As before, whenever there are too many aircraft overhead we set out for our stream—a three hours' march in the jungle! The forest is full of people: whistles, calls, and meetings.

The water is cold but no matter. During the first days only a very sketchy wash was possible. My first bath was in the muddy water of a rice field. I stopped our little column at nightfall and whether they objected or not, I had a bath. Co made this easy by standing guard. I get the impression that she doesn't like me very much. She is brusque, too brusque. I was wearing 'European' trousers while I waited for my pyjamas to dry, when all of a sudden she spat at my feet. Out of disgust for the tight-fitting trousers, perhaps to her a symbol of capitalism, or simply out of pure feminine jealousy?

We spend the days stretched out in hammocks. I try to improve my Vietnamese, and we look for snails which we then cook with rice. I read, we all read, then we sleep. It is pure *far niente* and almost a holiday existence, a holiday which might be anywhere in the world if it were not for these black pyjamas, these weapons and the jets diving over our heads. They drop their bombs very close to us. We can almost see the pilot.

Saturday, January 28

Six hours' marching a day! We were still in the house this morning when a Morane, then two, began to circle overhead.

Into the rice field, into the bushes, into the jungle, we made off at the double, almost running. My feet were bare—I didn't have time to put on my boots—but I scarcely felt the pain. I had only one thought: 'It's crazy to run. If they spot us from up there, we'll be shot down.'

By the time we reached the river, my feet were bleeding. White Teeth gave me his Ho Chi Minh sandals, which have already made the journey from Bong Son to Hanoi and back. Made of old tyres, with thongs on top, they are almost a symbol of the revolutionary army. I have adopted them and will never take them off again. Lighter and healthier than boots, they do not irritate the feet like socks that are continually wet through.

If a pair of tweezers keeps you from becoming a female monkey, they're also a pleasant way of passing the time: highly recommended for a desert island!

In the afternoon a new Co arrived with a present: a blanket! Everyone smiled happily at my surprise. She is much gentler than Co No. 1. As for the Beatles, they have gone, I think, for good.

Last night I went—hunting! It was all so unexpected and so incredible that I wonder whether anybody will believe my stories when I return. If I do return!

Lying in his hammock, Lynx Eye was preparing his equipment: pocket lamp fastened to his forehead by an elastic band, a strip of white paper stuck along the barrel of his rifle. In spite of my poor vocabulary, I was so insistent that he let me set out with him towards midnight.

At the end of the rice field, we waited for two hours, watching, without speaking, without moving, in the cold. In the end, we came back empty handed . . . and frozen!

Today we have had more luck: we stayed 'at home', as air traffic was giving us some peace, when all of a sudden we heard shouts and cries. Everyone rushed outside. A fox was asleep in the paddy! It took them half an hour to get him with stones and sticks. It made me sick to see it.

Two hours later there was a feast. It was as near as could be to delicious, and I forgot my disgust.

For the first time, during the killing, the thought came to me in a flash: 'What if I escaped now!'

I have discarded my mirror as no longer an essential in my life, but the lid of the milk tin could be used for signalling if I needed it. On one of the hills, almost at the top, I'm intrigued by three enormous clumps of rock, balancing there. They could make a hiding place. But the forests, the hills are inhabited: there are eyes everywhere. I would be found immediately.

And then, despite the doubts that overwhelm me sometimes, deep inside me I am confident: I prefer to wait and see.

Monday, January 30

No game of cards tonight. Since morning the battle has been raging on the other side of the mountain. We can see the planes, jets dive-bombing and when it's dark, the red trails of the tracer bullets from the 'dragon ships' (adapted Dakotas, with machine-guns firing from the portholes at the rate of 20,000 bullets a minute!).

No one spoke; no one slept, either. At two o'clock everyone got up. They killed a chicken, Co cooked it, and someone else went to hide my belongings. With the inevitable roll of rice round our necks, knapsacks on our backs and rifles slung over our shoulders, we set out, Co and I carrying a casserole between us.

This time we did not stop at the stream, but went farther on to a shelter in the middle of an enormous group of rocks—the lair of a tiger, if I understood correctly. Observation planes flew overhead incessantly. It was very cold, and we were shivering, but we jumped up and down to warm ourselves. It was raining, too, and we had to spend the night there.

Had the Americans already landed in our zone among the rice fields?

About midnight there was a raid of B-52s quite near, and I had the horrible feeling that everything was going to collapse around us, that we were going to be buried under an avalanche of rocks. The night seemed endless. If the sun shone in the morning, we were not aware of it; the vegetation was too dense.

In the afternoon a messenger appeared: we could go back. On the way we gathered wood for the fire. And so it was with our arms loaded that we arrived at last, exhausted. The children came running: 'Co, Co, Co, Michèle! Cam len!'

In spite of my weariness, I swung them round and tossed them up in the air. They laughed, and I was happy. I felt as if I'd come 'home'.

As usual, they were wearing nothing but a scrap of shirt, their stomachs and behinds bare. When the cold is more piercing than usual, their mother adds . . . a scarf around their heads!

I have been adopted; I live like a Vietnamese. By gestures and with the help of drawings they explained to me today:

'If you stay with us for ten years, eating rice, you are going to have slit eyes, a turned-up nose, black hair, and a brown skin.'

That would be quite a feat, wouldn't it? Perhaps I'd then be another Tron Thi Dao, able to halt 2,000 G.I.s!

Wednesday, February 1

In spite of some objections on the part of White Teeth—my independence and my little rebellions worry him—I went with the women to thin out rice plants. It was hard in the beginning, but then I got the knack. We laughed together, though we didn't understand each other. But gradually, as my thighs began to ache, I could feel my smile glazing. I admired their slender figures, their long, muscular legs with trousers rolled up to the top of their thighs and not a trace of skin disease. Alongside theirs, my white skin looked sickly.

They were indefatigable. By evening I was exhausted, ready to collapse on my bed, but they were still able to crush the rice, helped by three friendly young soldiers who were trying to make themselves useful. They had been there two days to recuperate—one of them was burning with fever. He had no medicine, nothing. I gave him my last two 'Aspro' and an anti-malaria tablet in some hot tea. He needed it more than I did. I've got thinner, certainly, but I feel strong and, up to a point, at the top of my form.

I am no longer frightened by the thought of a journey to Hanoi: it even begins to attract me—so many interesting things to see, to learn about.

Hanoi? Or to be set free? If it were not for my family, I know which I would choose.

Friday, February 3

Co No. 1 has left us again. She said goodbye to me in her usual abrupt way. But I am beginning to understand that it is just her manner. It is still very cold at night. There are sudden storms, with gale-force winds. Last night when the bombing stopped, I thought I heard the pounding of surf on the shore. I must have been dreaming.

The boys cough and spit. The cold and the guns keep us from sleeping. Twice we've had to take to the shelters, where the dampness of the ground makes us feel even colder.

An intensive bombardment always means: 'Take care, my beauties, we are landing tomorrow.' It was still dark when everyone got up. No time to eat, we must get going. Co, White Teeth, our three soldier friends, and I. Lynx Eye hasn't been seen since last night. This time we did not go in the direction of the stream or of the shelter, but headed towards the pass. Through paddies, mud, forests, hills and stones, we moved swiftly. The pass was wide; there were a few open spaces and innumerable holes, shelters and tunnels.

Among all those soldiers—more than 200, perhaps—I found my friends, the farmers, again—the placid inhabitants of all the houses where I'd stayed. In the face of danger they were either carrying sacks of rice or helping to dig holes. It was a hive of industry or more exactly, an ant-hill. I did not know everyone, but everyone seemed to know me.

'Chao co, Michèle! Cam len! Good morning, Michèle!'

Just as I did a few weeks ago among the G.I.s, I had the impression now that in some way I was 'good for their morale'. I would like to think that it was true and that by my presence I helped them a little —so little though it may be: 'A representative of the Western world lived with them for three weeks, like a true Vietnamese, became acclimatized, admired them, and told them so.'

A hundred yards farther on and White Teeth disappeared into some trees, with a white flag showing above the tops of them. A Morane began to circle above us. Co pushed me into an anti-aircraft machine-gun nest. Everyone disappeared into shelters, into holes and tunnels. The bushes parted and White Teeth came back, panting. We must go down into the valley.

But I suddenly had terrible pains in my stomach, I thought I was going to faint. I must get hold of myself. This is not the moment to be sick. The trees are blurred, everything is getting darker and darker . . .

'Co! Anh! I am BLIND! . . .'

Even sitting on the ground, I was swaying . . . I moved my hand in front of my open eyes to make them understand: everything is black, I can't see anything!

White Teeth makes me smell his Chinese medicine. Camphor for blindness! He doesn't know what to do. He and Co each hold one of my hands, and I cling to theirs. I'm blind. I feel so ill, I think I'm going to die. I'm so far from everything I know. I can't help thinking of the French Vice-Consul, Bion. Now it seems as though my search for him was a premonition.

I am sure I'm going to die.

The first bombs are falling—a mile and a half away perhaps. Whether by a mistake in calculation or through misinformation, they miss us. My ears are my only guide. Time seems like an eternity.

'Fifteen minutes,' Co told me later.

Then, as suddenly as it had happened, I could see again. A greyness, at first—Co and White Teeth were blurred. Then their images became clear and steady. The nightmare was over. I could SEE!

But I was still very weak. Helped and supported, I had to go on, down into the valley. My willpower got the upper hand again; I was ashamed of my weakness. We got there at last and stopped at the first house in the paddy. The bombing was still going on higher up.

I would have liked to lie down in the sun, but I had only a room without light, without a window, six feet by six, with the door shut. Co put up her hammock in the same room. I didn't understand. Was I a prisoner? I tried to protest, to get out, but weariness swept over me in waves, and I fell asleep. They brought me something to eat in the dark.

Then Lynx Eye reappeared. Every hour he came in to feel my forehead, and each one in turn brought me a banana, almost surreptitiously. Kindness, solicitude, but also these four walls! Why?

I rebelled and began to draft a letter to send off after the Têt cease-fire—and reached a firm decision, also.

'. . . for a month now, I have been the guest of the National Liberation Front. You must surely know that I am indeed Michèle Ray. I thought that the Têt, the truce, would have made my release easier. But I have had no word, nothing. I no longer consider myself a *guest*, but in fact a prisoner. As a member of the press, on these grounds, and as a sign of protest, I am today beginning a hunger strike . . . to continue until I am set free.'

That evening, with all outside doors shut, I went to eat with the others by the fire-side.

White Teeth and Lynx Eye never stopped teasing Co. Obviously they went too far, for she rushed out of the room in tears. I was furious and ticked them off in French, so they went after her and brought her back. There were no more tears!

We were all ready for the inevitable card game. This house was larger and more comfortable than the previous ones. Three rooms. No hammocks slung up tonight but beds everywhere, or mats on the floor.

There was a sound outside. Someone was coming. I was pulled and pushed into my room. Through the cracks in the boards I saw a Vietnamese come in. Who was he? Why was I not allowed to see him? Was this the reason for my four walls? Several times before, they had asked me to stay inside the house when a peasant was passing by, alone. Were they afraid he might talk too much? I had the impression that they were.

I knew that the professor, White Teeth, and Lynx Eye were responsible to their superiors for my health and my life. But what were their orders if we were surprised by the G.I.s or by Government soldiers? To release me, or to shoot me down, and in the latter case, considering the friendly relations that existed between us all, now that they had adopted me, would they carry out their orders, or would they hesitate?

18

Free!

Sunday, February 5

I am no longer shut up indoors; but in the sun, sitting in front of of the house. A little girl of ten, with a round face and mischievous eyes, as like as two peas to my niece, Christiane, brushes my hair and arranges it in two plaits.

While I was grating coconuts with the women, an uninterrupted line of soldiers and porters passed about 150 yards away. They had come down from the pass and were heading towards the other side of the valley. Were they going to the valley of An Lao, one of their strongholds?

Perhaps yesterday's bombing attained its objective and they were moving headquarters.

'But that is my friend, the professor!' I fell into his arms. At last I could speak French again!

I began to fume:

'I thought I was a guest. Yesterday I was a prisoner.'

He laughed and introduced me to the man responsible to the N.L.F. for the province of Binh Dinh. Thirty-five to forty years old, he was wearing a beige uniform with a Colt at his belt. The revolver is obviously a symbol of authority. It also states just as clearly, 'I've had the hide of an American to get this for myself.'

'I have a surprise for you,' the professor announced.

Everyone stared at me attentively.

'We are taking you back close to Tam Quan tonight and will set you free tomorrow morning. We intended to do it during Têt, to take advantage of the truce, but you have been sick. We're afraid that Hanoi is not possible; much too arduous and exhausting a journey. But go there through Cambodia by plane. And don't forget to go and see my sister,' he reminded me.

I didn't know what to say. Set free? The words didn't seem to have much meaning for me. But my luck went even further.

MH

'The puppet troops have found your car. It must be at Bong Son.'

Smiling, I showed the professor the letter I had prepared. My letter of rebellion.

'You doubted us . . .' A shadow passed over his face.

I tried to explain my moment of depression due to being far away from my family, and to their anxiety over me.

'I gave you a month to get information about me. When the time was up, I would no longer have been in doubt, but certain—that for no valid reason, I would never be set free.'

'I understand. We, too, in the mountains, often think sadly of our own people, our families who are so far away. You are not going to Hanoi, but we admire you greatly just the same for your willingness, your courage, and above all for your good nature.'

The head of the province was the same as all the others. After ten minutes, he brought out his wallet and showed me photos of his family, his children, and Ho Chi Minh. The same thing had happened on the other side. With one difference, nevertheless: what G.I. would go around with a photo of President Johnson!

On a sudden impulse he suggested, 'Keep the photo of Ho Chi Minh as a souvenir.' But Uncle Ho's beard had stuck to the plastic cover. 'I'm sorry! I'll try to find you another one!'

Ho Chi Minh without his beard is not Ho Chi Minh!

Goodbye, Co! I gave her my last necklace. Goodbye, 'Christiane!' The children crowded around me and followed me for several hundred yards. It was a fine day, the valley was broad, the sky was blue, the rice field was beautiful. The coconut palms, the women planting out the rice, and others we met, trotting along the road, their balancing-poles on their shoulders, and children running, playing. All of them gave us wide smiles. But I could read astonishment on their faces. 'A white partisan! And so tall!'

Two carpenters were working on a doorstep. 'Bonjour, Monsieur!' they called to me, waving their hands.

Not a sound, no guns. It was almost peaceful. It was so beautiful.

Farther on, as we moved along the side of a mountain, we saw several houses burned by napalm, and bomb craters everywhere. War had been there, but today it seemed to be forgotten.

In a bright house whose walls had been whitewashed—no doubt for the Têt—a magnificent feast was waiting for us, a luxury to which I had become quite unaccustomed! A table and benches and perhaps twenty bowls all set out in a row, all filled with different foods. For drinks we had whole coconuts. Dozens of laughing eyes, both curious and moved, were watching me. They were happy at my surprise. Little by little, the whole village came in. I was no longer just an object of curiosity—I was one of them.

We all talked at the same time, the professor acting as interpreter. There was an atmosphere of great excitement, which surely hid a certain nostalgia. I was given presents: pamphlets with dedications written on them, a bowl for rice made from a napalm container, a flag of the National Liberation Front.

'It dates from 1960. Perhaps the Thieu-Ky people will want to take it from you. Try to keep everything in memory of the Front, of your three weeks here, of our comrades who have become your friends.'

'What are you going to do, go on with your journey? If you are arrested again, you will have to spend another three weeks in the mountains for identification!' That possibility seemed to amuse them!

'Give me a pass.'

'That will not prevent you being detained while they check on the pass. No, come back during the Têt next Thursday to the place where you were intercepted by our soldiers. We will keep watch over the road. We are having a big festival, a theatrical troop. The *Thieu-Ky* soldiers are coming, too, but unarmed. It's a fraternization. You'll probably see your friends, the peasants from the mountain, who are coming down for it. The next day we will put you in the care of a motor-cyclist who will take you as far as Quang Ngai, where you can have your car sent by plane! But don't come back after that, and take care! There is a Vietnam proverb that says, "If you go out too often in the night, one day you'll see ghosts", and we would be upset if anything happened to you.'

Our little reunion lasted for two or three hours. Another meal, more celebrations. Then the artillery began. Quick, into the shelter! For the last time, I hoped. I was between two women with babies at their breasts. We smiled at each other. By the time it was over, the dinner was cold.

'My colleagues, my journalist friends from Saigon, are going to tell me, "Of course you were set free! You are a Frenchwoman."

If I was an American and had undertaken the same journey, would my fate have been different?'

'No,' replied the head of the province. 'The work of a journalist is to see: you have seen, a little, you have suffered like us under the bombardments. If you were American, we would also set you free. I will go farther: I invite to Binh Dinh, to my province, any journalist who wants to come, American or French.'

I passed on the invitation. But so far, no one, I believe, has appeared on route No. 1 saying, 'Michèle told me that . . .'

I was given paper and a pen to write a 'declaration'—a declaration in which I was to certify that 'American imperialists kill women and children'. I felt too confident to believe that my freedom depended on signing it. I refused categorically.

I am just as much against the G.I.'s picture of the Vietcong as the Vietcong's picture of the G.I. Both are false; and both are propaganda, the propaganda of a country at war, which must make the enemy into a monster, and never a human being.

Because I wanted to, because I felt an urge to do so, I wrote them a letter, which was addressed to the head of the province, but which was, in fact, for all my friends, for all those I had met. I thanked them—not for having captured me—but for having been true to the picture I had formed of them before I left Ca Mau, for letting me share their lives and their fears, and for helping me to understand a little better the reason for their resistance. 'If I were Vietnamese I would not be Vietcong, but an N.L.F. partisan, an ardent nationalist.'

I don't think I wrote all they would have liked me to, but I felt that my letter touched them, perhaps simply because it came from me, of my own free will, and was not exacted from me.

Before we set out on the last march, Lynx Eye rose, very ceremoniously, and very moved.

'We are happy for you, because you're going back to your own life, to Patrick, to your family. We have not the slightest hope of ever seeing you again. We've become used to you, and have learned to think of you as one of us.'

The professor had the last word:

'If you go to Hanoi, go and see my sister. Some day when the war is finished at last, come back. I invite you to my house for as long as you please. With Patrick, of course.'

Moved and deeply touched, I left them there. I went off alone with White Teeth and the head of the province.

The night was black, without a moon, but we didn't dare to strike a light. Walking single file along a narrow path bordered with sharp, poisoned stakes, I could scarcely distinguish the tiny reflection of light on the cone-shaped hat ahead of me. When it became specially difficult the two men gave me their hands. With all my senses alert, I struggled to penetrate the darkness. Fear of falling into the holes made my balance uncertain. But that was just as well: my mind was occupied, I had no time to think.

6 o'clock in the morning
Monday, February 6

We arrived at route No. 1 and stopped at last about a hundred yards from the road. There was breakfast of rice, chicken, and bananas, while the two boys of the house—about fourteen years old —played the guitar. I gave White Teeth his receipt, and he returned all my belongings. Nothing at all was missing, except for a few little things I had given away myself.

I left them one of my cameras, the easiest one to work, as a souvenir. White Teeth was wild with joy. He gave me his name and address at Bong Son and asked me to send him my newspaper articles. But in case his letters are opened and they arrest him for it, I shan't do so.

On route No. 1, the only means of transport are bicycles or auto-cycles, so overloaded that they're top-heavy. It seemed an eternity since I flew over this road with Colonel Bush.

An auto-cycle driver had been given orders to take me to Tam Quan, either to the Government authorities or to the Americans.

'I would rather go on foot. I don't want to make any trouble for him.'

'His civilian papers are in order, and he has a written order signed by the Front. *They* won't say anything to him. They know he has to obey, to avoid reprisals. It is our policy to protect the people who help us,' the professor had explained to me, laughing, the evening before. 'We trust you, too, to help him get out of trouble, if necessary.'

I sat down on the luggage carrier. It's always difficult to say goodbye. I've never known how to do it. With language difficulties, it's even worse. In any case, what could I say? Thank you for capturing me? Thank you for letting me go? Thank you for my holiday . . .? 'Goodbye' or 'Till next time'? How could I sum up the powerful emotions of that three weeks' experience? I couldn't say a word. I just waved my hand and tears streamed down my face.

Five hundred yards farther on, we came to a river. The bridge had been blown up, but a temporary crossing of sampans had been laid on with a toll station for the Front: five piastres for passengers, ten for auto-cyclists. I did not pay: they were expecting me.

With all of us crowded into the sampan, a Vietnamese girl tried to speak a little broken English. I answered her very proudly in Vietnamese. Words flew back and forth: 'Vietcong . . . *Phap* . . . *My* . . .'

On 'the other side', yet another 500 yards, and still riding on the luggage-carrier, I waved my hand to the soldiers of Ky. Two hundred yards more, and we were in Tam Quan. I arrived in the village square at market time: a sea of cone-shaped hats. There my driver left me—brave but not reckless!

The crowd, the noise, my head whirling.

'Michèle Ray?' A Vietnamese lieutenant who spoke French took my knapsack. Still surrounded by a crowd, we went towards a hut.

'Michèle! Here you are! My God!'

I fell into the arms of the American sergeant and the camp doctor. 'I'm terribly sorry but I have to check your luggage,' the young lieutenant in charge of security told me. He was very embarrassed.

I let him do it, confident that I was not a messenger of death. Major Porter came to get me in his helicopter. And only then did I begin to realize that I was 'on the other side'. The noise that had made me jump for three long weeks, that helicopter that had represented danger, was now only a means of transport.

'A means of transport, Michèle!'

It was fine, though a little misty. In the valley, I caught sight of the bomb craters, the 'sieve'. My tears began to flow, faster and faster: I couldn't prevent them, I sobbed. I tried to stop. I didn't want anyone to see me crying, and above all I didn't want sympathy. No one would understand.

I know that, in spite of my promise, I won't be able to go to the

New Year's rendezvous. I won't be able to take the professor extra
lenses for his glasses, or the music of French folk songs—or anything.
I know I'll be breaking my word, and I'm reproaching myself
already. But I've come back to my own world, and I must accept
its demands. As Lynx Eye said, 'You are leaving us. It's a total
parting, it's like death. . . .' Yes, it's a total parting.

At Bong Son, they were all there to welcome me! Tommy
Waugh—I'd said to him as I left camp that day: 'I'm coming back
in half an hour . . . I hope!': Jerry Hanson, the best amateur cook:
Captain John McCloskey.

'Thank you, John.'

'What for?'

'If you'd taken me with you on patrol that morning, I would have
left at two o'clock on the Caribou.'

'So it's my fault?'

'Not at all! It was a combination of circumstances. Happy circumstances, as I've come back again. I've had the most staggering,
the most moving, the most interesting experience of my life.'

Lieutenant Colonel Nguyen Long and the 42nd Regiment
invited me for Têt—they, too!

Accompanied by Major Jones, P.I.O. of the First Cavalry
division, we took another helicopter and landed at Hammond, the
headquarters of two brigades of the First Cavalry.

'Well, Michèle! You kept my special plane waiting!' said Colonel
Wolf with a laugh.

My picture was taken in front of the divisional sign of the First
Cavalry, and in front of the helicopters, with the officers and men
always posing slightly sideways—watch those medals!

A light lunch, but I couldn't swallow anything. My stomach was
too tense. And so I let myself be led wherever they wanted to take
me, caught up in a whirlwind.

I was questioned—with Coca Cola—for more than three hours in
the G2 Intelligence Officer's tent. Among other things, they were
trying to identify the various places I'd been. The maps danced
before my eyes. Villages became faces, voices, laughter—and also
fear. I felt crushed by the weight of America. Outside, the incessant
noise of helicopters still didn't exactly reassure my ears.

'You know Bong Son–English well. Were you questioned about
our installations?'

'Never. They have more confidence in their intelligence agents than in a woman, I suppose.'

Did he understand? I explained further: 'I kept a diary that was never inspected, even when I wasn't there.'

Major Jones, who had been hovering about solicitously, broke up the session and took me to the doctor.

'Take these two tablets. That will relax you.'

He listened briefly to my lungs. 'Cough.'

'Were you forced?'

I didn't understand, and I looked at him in astonishment.

'Did they abuse you?'

I burst out laughing, but I really wanted to cry.

Yes, I am really on 'the other side'. White Teeth, Lynx Eye, the Beatles, the professor . . . they've all become Vietcong again, 'Victor Charlie', a vague black mass, shifting and impersonal . . . the Enemy.

PART IV

Conclusion

19

Exit from Hell

Hong Kong, March 1, 1967
My dear Pat,
I am in Hong Kong for a week. I need a transition period before returning to France, before returning home after seven months in Vietnam, on the two shores of hell. And then, I must admit it, I'm frightened. Yes, frightened of the questions, and of my replies. Frightened, too, that my capture might become, after a while, almost a legend and no longer a very real and deep emotional experience, that it might become a story like any other. Have you read in *The New York Times* what Saigon officials have to say about my journey to 'the other side'? Here is a comment by Jack Stuart of the 'five o'clock follies': 'The Vietcong knew who she was and they have been very cunning. They used her to make propaganda for themselves.'

Those same officials shrugged their shoulders when, as I set out on my journey, I said to them, 'After all, danger is relative. I consider "Victor Charlie" intelligent.' And now when I tell them that—in Binh Dinh where one of their élite units, the First Cavalry division, operates—I saw soldiers of the N.L.F. or of the regular North Vietnamese army, apparently in fine shape with excellent morale, a people who live and work under incessant bombardment, who have, in a way, become used to it, but who can laugh, joke, and go on living. . . . All that contradicts the reports of the Rand Corporation's electronic computers with their perforated cards certifying that 'The morale of the Vietcong is poor. He lives in constant terror of being bombed.'

In other words, in speaking of the professor or of White Teeth, I made the enemy sound like a human being. They won't forgive me for that. To make the enemy human is high treason. He must remain 'Victor Charlie', sly, cruel, and sadistic. And what of the American as the Vietcong sees him? A ruthless imperialist who burns women and children, and eats them, too! Yes, I said 'eats them'!

Those two images are the result of a war propaganda that has to show the enemy to be everything evil. Everything except a human being, an individual.

During my last week in Vietnam, whether it was spent among American officers or with new drafts, the questions were always the same:

'Can you explain how *they* can be so aggressive, so dedicated, whereas on this side they frankly don't want to fight? And yet they are the same people!'

Sometimes they also ask, 'Why aren't *they* the ones we are advising?'

Since my return, I have been subjected to a number of petty official annoyances that are normally reserved for people who do not follow the official line.

François Nivolon, the correspondent of *Figaro* in Saigon, went with me to the Immigration Office to help me to get an exit visa. The official, a middle-aged man in civilian clothes, insisted that I give him a handwritten account of the circumstances of my capture and what I thought of the Vietcong.

After reading my report, he said, 'And now we must have another declaration certifying that you did not sign any papers when you were with the Vietcong, promising to write articles in their favour.'

I burst out laughing.

'And suppose I say that I did? What will happen?'

'. . . Well, I don't know!'

The decision then would not have rested with him, but would have had to 'go higher up'.

In any case at the same time he was winding up a long discussion with Nivolon—about his family in France and his ambition to get a post abroad, adding: 'And then! *Ciao!* They wouldn't see me again!' Which was not lacking in a certain humour after he'd made me write all those declarations.

How was my stay in the Grall Hospital, you ask?

Apart from loss of weight—eleven pounds—and a lack of vitamins B_1 and B_6, the doctors found me 'in perfect shape', in spite of having spent three weeks in the jungle, at the height of the rainy season. The training I had with the G.I.s had something to do with it, I think. With the 'Viets' I lost the extra pounds I'd put on eating C-rations! An excellent slimming diet!

I try to joke, but in fact my heart's not in it. My morale's at zero. It seems to me that the shock of returning is greater than the shock of being captured.

For three weeks I lived like a Vietnamese, in a territory held by the N.L.F. I ate and slept with them, and like them, I was frightened. For three weeks the Americans became the enemy.

I may know nothing about politics—the policies of Hanoi, of Washington, or of Peking—but on the human side I have always thought of the G.I.s as friends. Perhaps because I understand their problems, their difficulties, their suffering.

But I've never identified myself with them as I did with the Vietcong during those three weeks. Perhaps because the Americans are not over-enthusiastic about this war, they did not succeed in making me share a faith they do not have. They are doing a job of work, and they do it well. That's all.

After my release, at English, at Hammond, or at An Khê, I had moments of wanting to protest, to block my ears, to see no more of them. They were a mass, a ruthless force. I was shattered—the transition was too brutal. I hated them, I felt sick inside, and I was ashamed of feeling like it.

Because for three weeks I was able to identify myself with 'Victor Charlie', because for three weeks I was absorbing something of the intensity of his feelings which would suddenly come to the surface, I could better understand the tremendous determination of these men whether they're labelled Communists or nationalists.

You know—or don't know—that before I was released, and of my own free will, I gave them a letter. To thank them for having been intelligent, as Jack Stuart says, but also to tell them that had I been a Vietnamese, I would have fought on their side.

I would not be a Communist, but fiercely nationalist—the N.L.F. would represent the only decent, honourable solution. Even though I know that, despite its appearance of representing all parties, the intricate machinery and the leadership of the N.L.F. are in the hands of the Communists.

How can one believe in the South Vietnamese government, rotten at every level, or in Ky, in that 'puppet army', to use the Vietcongs' favourite expression? That army which would make me ashamed to be a Vietnamese?

The peasant, the *nha-quê* of the Delta, whom I knew is not Communist, either. He is too lazy, too individualistic, with a deep sense of family. In fact, he wants only one thing: to cultivate his fields in peace. And he wants peace at any price—whether it be white or red, whether the bowl of rice is named Ky or Ho Chi Minh. Why else does he help the Vietcong, when he is not forced to do so?

Apart from a question of honour, perhaps it all comes down to a question of skin as well—as the planter in the highlands told an American journalist who reproached him for being 'pro-Vietcong'.

The Ky bowl of rice is in fact labelled Johnson—a Johnson who wants to save the peasant from Communism by unloading on him daily a hundred tons of napalm and two hundred tons of bombs. Nobody wants to be saved at such a price!

When John Steinbeck, during his visit to Vietnam, told an American journalist in Da Nang: 'Wars are needed to make men . . .', I felt disgusted—sad, too, because I liked Steinbeck. But for all those who have admired him, didn't he die after writing *Letters to Alicia*, his experiences in Vietnam when he followed the G.I.s, a grenade on his belt, and an M.16 in his hand?

The war in Vietnam is producing a type of fighting man different from those America has so far known—unless I have always had the wrong idea of American democracy. Young Americans face a contradiction between the idealist education they've received and the rationalized war into which they have been plunged.

In the name of what, in support of what ideal? To defend whom? A conception of America's place in the world. But what conception?

They are not used to finding themselves on the wrong side of the barricade, and so they try to work off their complexes by adopting a professional, mercenary attitude of killers.

My testimony is sure to be distorted, denounced and criticized by this one and that. Even so, I wanted to tell what I saw, lived through and felt. I wanted to add my statement to the drama in which I became involved, not only as a woman, but as a French woman, in theory neutral.

But can one remain neutral in a war? I have taken up a position, but I'm torn in two. . . . Perhaps just because I've had a worm's eye view of it.

I'll therefore leave the political analysis to the experts in Washington, Hanoi, Paris, Saigon and Peking. I only know—well—the human side, and I know that this Vietnam is going to haunt me for a long time to come. Until the end of the war. But when will that be?

Glossary

A.B.C.	American Broadcasting Company
A.F.P.	Agence France-Presse
A.R.V.N.	Army of the Republic of Vietnam
C.B.C.	Columbia Broadcasting Corporation
C.I.D.G.	Civil Irregular Defence Group
F.A.C.	Forward Aircraft Control
J.U.S.P.A.O.	Joint United States Public Affairs Office
L.L.D.B.	Luc Luong Dac Biet (Vietnamese Special Forces)
M.A.C.V.	Military Assistant Command in Vietnam
N.L.F.	National Liberation Front
P.I.O.	Press Information Office/Officer
U.S.O.M.	United States Operation Mission
V.C.	Vietcong (in radio messages it becomes Victor Charlie)

VELLEIUS PATERCULUS

COMPENDIUM OF ROMAN HISTORY

RES GESTAE DIVI AUGUSTI

WITH AN ENGLISH TRANSLATION BY

FREDERICK W. SHIPLEY

HARVARD UNIVERSITY PRESS
CAMBRIDGE, MASSACHUSETTS
LONDON, ENGLAND

First published 1924
Reprinted 1955, 1961, 1967, 1979, 1992, 1998

LOEB CLASSICAL LIBRARY® is a registered trademark
of the President and Fellows of Harvard College

ISBN 0-674-99168-0

Printed in Great Britain by St Edmundsbury Press Ltd,
Bury St Edmunds, Suffolk, on acid-free paper.
Bound by Hunter & Foulis Ltd, Edinburgh, Scotland.